KV-590-856

A GUIDE TO CREATIVE TUTORING

Kogan Page Books for Teachers series
Series Editor: Tom Marjoram

A GUIDE TO CREATIVE TUTORING

THE TUTOR ASCENDANT

— Stephen Adams —

Books for Teachers
Series Editor: Tom Marjoram

KOGAN PAGE

First published in 1989 by
Kogan Page Ltd
120 Pentonville Road, London N1 9JN

British Library Cataloguing in Publication Data

Adams, Stephen
  A guide to creative tutoring: the tutor ascendant
  (Books for teachers).
  1. Great Britain. Schools. Students. Counselling
  I. Title   II. Series
  371.4'0941

  ISBN 1-85091-832-5
      0000706
Typeset by DP Photosetting, Aylesbury, Bucks
Printed and bound in Great Britain by
Biddles Ltd, Guildford

370.33
ADA

Contents

A Note on Terminology

I should explain two points of style which are intentional. First, I need to explain my use of gender. The practice in the past has been to use the masculine pronouns 'he', 'his', 'him', when referring to either sex. Recently, there has been a move, which I approve, towards using the feminine gender in a similar way. However, there are advantages to a practice which employs both genders to assist in avoiding ambiguity. What I am doing in this book, therefore, is using the masculine gender to indicate the tutor, and the feminine gender when referring to all other parties. Thus, pastoral middle management, deputy heads and heads are all female, and so are parents and students.

Many of the tutors in my own team have been female, so using the masculine gender is a reminder to me that they are frequently male. The application of the feminine gender to senior teaching staff will, I hope, be a minor contribution to increasing the recognition that women can occupy such posts. That students who misbehave are stereotyped as male seems to me unfortunate and using the feminine gender unless there is a specific point to be made seems helpful in attacking this myth. I regret that I shall contribute to the expectation that the mother rather than the father will be the parent who has the responsibility for contacting the school, when the benefits of both parents being involved and displaying a united front are manifest, but the advantages in dealing with ambiguity seem to me to outweigh that defect. I hope that the reader will not be offended by any of this usage.

Second, I have deliberately and consistently employed the word 'student' in preference to 'pupil' or 'child'. This is as a result of feelings of my own, but confirmed in discussion with an English class, many of whom objected to 'pupil' most strongly. The problem which it causes is that it can be ambiguous if there is any mention of student teachers, but where this is the case I have been explicit. Many teachers use 'kid' ubiquitously, but my English group were even more antipathetic to this word, which certainly looks disparaging on the printed page.

Acknowledgements

First and foremost, I must thank Roy Pearce, Head Teacher of Anthony Gell School, Wirksworth, for his support, training and encouragement over nine years – and indeed to spotting something in a grammar school assistant English teacher which caused him to appoint me as Head of Gell House in the first place. It is the simple truth to say: *sine qua non*.

Secondly, I have to thank Derbyshire LEA for seconding me for one year during which I was able to write this book. The Education Committee's vision and commitment is an encouragement for those of us who teach within the county.

Third, I want to thank all those teachers and trainers with whom I have worked this year. I make no distinction between the teachers and trainers since both have influenced me equally. I would, however, like to thank specifically Barbara Pearce of CCDU at Leeds University for allowing me to join the CCDU 'Training the Trainers' course, and Jane Falk of the University of Nottingham School of Education for all her help and encouragement. Both have been very influential and have made the writing of Chapter 3 in particular possible.

Fourth, I need to thank all those who have read parts of the book, made suggestions and given advice, information, and encouragement – in particular, Heather Kinsella, Alec Rapkin, Cheryl Richardson, Dave Robson, Joe Theaker, Terry Woodcock and Arthur Wooster, and especially my father, Fred Adams, who read most of it at all stages.

Finally, I would like to thank the staff and students of Fearne and Gell Houses, with whom I have worked and from whom I have learnt, and especially my successive Assistant Heads of House, Anne Hall and Alan Brown, whose loyalty and support was unstinted.

Introduction

The most common use of the term 'tutor' in secondary schools, and the one to which I shall adhere in this book, is to refer to that role of the teacher which places her/him in charge of a group of young people as part of the pastoral structure. The perception of the tutor's function varies according to the view of pastoral care taken by the school. Traditionally, the form teacher – from whom the tutor is descended – is the first person to whom the student relates and the person who has the immediate responsibility for the day-to-day discipline of the student. The role of the tutor, like everything else in a dynamic education system, is constantly changing, affected by developments in educational thinking, but at present a median position would probably perceive the tutor as in some sense having the responsibility to 'look after' the members of the group as a kind of surrogate parent.

The tutor will be a member – at least in theory – of a team of tutors within a larger unit. Most commonly, this unit is a year, which means that all members of the team will have groups of students of the same age. Thus, you may be a second-year tutor, in which case your tutor group will consist of second-year students, and the other members of the tutor team will also have second-year groups. The team will be under the leadership of a head of year, who will probably be regarded as middle management, and be paid on a similar scale to that of a head of a large or small department, depending on the status accorded to pastoral care in the school and on the number of students in each year.

The year structure is known as a horizontal system. Horizontal systems can be 'rolling' or 'static' or a combination of the two. A rolling system is one where the tutor team move up each year with their tutor groups. The second-year tutor was thus a first-year tutor last year and will be a third-year tutor next year. This gives continuity of care, since a student will stay with the same tutor for the duration of her/his time in the school, unless the tutor leaves or a decision is taken to transfer the student for some reason. If the tutors and year head remain as, for example, second-year tutors and head of second year while the students move up, so that they take over a new second year each year, the system will be static. It is possible to have a system where the tutors roll but the head of year remains to be an expert on that particular stage of school life, or even where the head of year alone rolls, thus becoming the element of continuity, so that she/he is able to maintain knowledge of and contact with the same group of children.

An alternative model is a vertical or house system. The school is divided across the whole five or seven years, so that students enter a particular house in the first year and remain in it until they leave. Within the house, the tutor groups can be horizontal – that is, each group will have students of the same age but all will be members of the same house – or vertical. This latter is sometimes known as the 'family group' model, since within the tutor group will be students of all ages, just as in a family. Verticality gives continuity of care, since a tutor in a vertical tutor group will take in a small number of first-year students to join the older students already there. Horizontal groups within a house can and usually do roll, as in the rolling horizontal system.

There are other systems, but they are generally variations on the two systems outlined above. Whatever the structure, the precise nature of the role of the tutor will vary greatly, according to the philosophy of the school.

As a pastoral care trainer and a Head of House, it has been impossible for me to be unaware that the vast majority of new teachers in secondary schools come into the job with little – often no – training for the pastoral work that almost all are expected to do. They have applied for the job as a subject teacher, and yet they find that this is only part of the role they are to fulfil. They are also to be a tutor – a more or less demanding and responsible role within the pastoral sysem.

There *are* colleges and university departments of education which provide courses in pastoral care, but those which make them a compulsory part of the curriculum are rare, and yet the job of tutor is almost never optional.

Some schools make an effort to correct this omission, often by asking the new teacher to be an assistant tutor to an experienced tutor, so that the job can be learnt by helping with the work of the tutor, by taking on specific tasks or specific students, and all the time having someone to monitor and consult with.

Some LEAs make provision for pastoral training as part of the induction programmes which they organise for probationers. Others offer courses to teachers who have been in the job for a year or so, at which time their needs are clearer to them.

However, many new tutors feel that they are not at all prepared for the role. They are not clear about how to do the tasks which are clearly within their brief; the particular relationships which they find to be necessary are difficult to characterise and even more difficult to establish; they feel that they lack the skills to handle the situations which arise; and they are unclear about just how far their responsibilities stretch.

The purpose of this book is, first and foremost, to provide for these needs. It will lead the new tutor from the most basic tasks through to those requiring sensitivity and skill. But there is also a second purpose and that is to offer a view of the role of the tutor within a secondary school which places the tutor at the centre of the pastoral system, rather than on the periphery as is sometimes felt to be the case.

Through this means, the job of the tutor can be seen as demanding, responsible and satisfying, rather than menial and tedious. From the point of view of the school – by which I mean not the authorities but the people who make up the institution – every tutor being engaged in pastoral work means that the care which is provided is far more comprehensive than if it is provided by a few designated 'pastoral teachers' who only have time to look after, at best, the children with obvious problems and at worst the children who *are* obvious problems.

To view all teachers as pastoral teachers is also to prevent a situation arising where most teachers regard anything beyond the confines of their academic discipline as being beyond their responsibility – a scenario which has become known as the 'pastoral-academic split' and involves the creation of a divide in the conception which teachers have concerning the nature and boundaries of their job, and a dilution of the sense of purpose of the institution.

A new tutor, like a new driver, may feel overawed by all the aspects of the job which have to be learnt, but in the end the kind of tutor who I am advocating – which Marland (1974) calls 'the ascendant tutor' – will find the job far more satisfying and fulfilling than those tutors who operate in schools where the tutor is seen as an administrative functionary who has to pass on anything requiring skill or sensitivity to someone else.

In planning the shape of the book, I have tried to approach the different aspects of the job in order of urgency. I have begun with the basic needs of the tutor, the tasks which *have* to be done by the tutor in virtually any secondary school, to achieve what I call minimal tutoring. These are administrative tasks, handling the basic organisation of the tutor group, and monitoring the progress and coping capacity of the students within the group.

Chapter 2 examines the notion of tutor ascendancy, and explores the nature of the relationships which the tutor needs to establish with his tutees, with their parents, with his pastoral head, and with other staff, to further most satisfactorily the objective of providing full care for tutees.

In Chapter 3, I describe some methods which the tutor can employ to build a sense of unity, identity and mutual support within a group, and other activities which can occupy the structured tutorial time which is now part of the timetable of most secondary schools.

Chapter 4 is about the various sources of help which are available both inside and outside the school, and when and how they should be utilised. Whether or not the tutor finds himself actually undertaking this kind of liaison will depend on the role which he is allowed, but even if he does not, he may benefit from an awareness of the functions of the helping agencies and the way in which they can be exploited in the interests of his tutees.

Chapter 5 is concerned with the skills needed to work one-to-one with a student who asks for help with a problem, often called counselling skills.

Chapter 6 looks at the variety of records, reports, references and profiles which need to be written by the tutor, and considers the role of the tutor in the process of reviewing and negotiation which will be involved when records of achievement are introduced nationally.

In Chapter 7, various problems are discussed which are associated with working in schools where the ethos of the institution, the line taken by the head teacher or the attitudes of the majority of other staff mean that an aspiring ascendant tutor will not be easily accommodated.

This is intended to be a practical book, so I have included material which can be used with groups of students or individuals. I have also included questionnaires intended for self-exploration which I hope will be useful in assessing the reader's own attitudes, learning and development.

Chapter 1

Minimal Tutoring: Survival as a New Tutor

Where are you now?

It is a principle of good practice in the classroom to begin an aspect of the curriculum by encouraging students to focus on the knowledge, experience and skills which they already have in that field. It is worth spending time finding out where, in other words, the student is now, and since the training of teachers should always endeavour to model the approaches which they are to use with their students, that is exactly where we shall start.

Schools vary considerably in the attitude they take to the tutor and consequently in the job they expect him to do. It is therefore the first task for the aspiring tutor to find out which sort of school he is in. What role does the tutor have? Michael Marland's role of the tutor indicator (Marland, 1974) as adapted by Clemett and Pearce (1986) in Table 1.1 is a useful way of assessing this.

First, look down the three columns. You will see that each line describes a different position on what we might call the pastoral care spectrum. Where does your school lie?

To take line A, is a tutor in your school expected to know everything that the school knows about the children in his tutor group? Or is the information kept (known) by someone in middle or senior management, like the head of year or a pastoral deputy head? If the latter is the case, can the tutor get the information if he requires it, or will the barriers come down if he asks, telling him that this information is 'confidential', or 'only available to senior staff', or whatever is felt to be the appropriate way of discouraging further enquiry?

Your school may straddle two columns. Some schools simply don't think of giving information to tutors about their tutees, but if the tutor asked for it the head of year, say, would be delighted to see evidence of

Table 1.1 *The Role of the Tutor Indicator*

	Tutor ascendant	Tutor neutral	Tutor subordinate
A	Tutor is obliged to have access to all information on pupils	Information mostly available on request	Tutor not given confidential information on pupils
B	Tutor vital part of admission and induction process	Tutor fully informed in advance that new pupils will arrive	New pupils sent to joint form group without prior notification
C	Subject teachers contact tutor in first instance, when worried	Subject teachers sometimes keep tutor in touch, but not always	Subject teachers always go to pastoral head in serious cases
D	Letters written home by tutor on his/her own initiative	Tutor can suggest letter required	Tutor not normally shown pastoral head's correspondence
E	Tutor basically responsible for attendance, calling for help when the need is felt	Pastoral head follows up absence queries initiated by tutor	Tutor merely marks absence in the register and takes no further action
F	Tutor plays major advisory part in vocational and educational decisions	Tutor's assessment noted in writing	All vocational and educational advice centralised
G	Tutor present at all major interviews with parents, careers, advisory, welfare officers etc	Tutor told what took place at the interview	Tutor not informed such interviews are to happen
H	Tutor's views usually solicited by senior staff before pupil seen by them	Tutor informed reasonably fully of any action by senior staff	Summary action taken by senior staff without notification to tutor
J	Tutor keeps responsibility for the group throughout their school career	Tutors may follow groups if they express strong wish to	Tutors assigned to forms on *ad hoc* basis or for administrative convenience
K	Tutor designs his/her own 'Pastoral Curriculum' within overall scheme	Intermediate position	Tutors given all worksheets etc and expected to 'do'. Or no 'pastoral curriculum'
L	Tutor feels the primary responsibility for his/her group's development	Tutor feels significant assistant in the P/Care process	Tutor feels basically a register checker

Adapted from Marland (1974) by John Pearce (1986) in *The Evaluation of Pastoral Care*. Reproduced by kind permission of John Pearce and Basil Blackwell Limited.

such interest and commitment from him. Also, whatever the avowed policy, or indeed the intention, of a school, in practice when everyone is rushed off their feet communication is far less free than everyone would like it to be, or it simply gets forgotten sometimes. This may happen in line B, for instance, when the management forget to involve or inform the tutor about a new pupil even when they intend that he should be involved.

But it is what really happens that counts. Schools are not what they say they are; they are what they actually do, so in your judgements here don't be influenced by what you have heard people in the school *say* happens.

I am not suggesting that once you have identified where your school lies in its view of the tutor's role you simply accept it. (I shall return to what you should do if you feel that your school places a lower status on the tutor in Chapters 2 and 7.) First, however, you need to know what the school's expectations are because that is where you must start, both in the sense that you can only extend your role when you know where you are extending it from, and also in the sense that you have to satisfy the school that you can do the job as they define it before you can go on to do anything more.

When you have been through the Indicator and established where your school lies, focus next on what role you would like the tutor to have if you could choose. Go through the Indicator again, this time thinking about your ideal school and what its view of the role of the tutor would be. For instance, in line G, would you want to be present at all major interviews with parents, careers advisers, welfare officers, etc? Or, in line H, would you want to be asked your views before a senior member of staff interviewed one of your tutees?

When you have been through the Indicator again, you will have some idea of whether there is a tension between the role you would like to have as a tutor and the role which tutors are expected to have in your school. Clearly, if the two coincide, you are unusually fortunate.

From the second chapter onwards, I shall base the training on the ascendant role since that way we shall cover all aspects of the tutor's job and because, as I shall argue, it is the most effective way to provide pastoral facilities for all students.

The training in this chapter, however, will aim to cover only what might be described as the least the tutor can get away with while still approaching the role responsibly and humanely. This is what I mean by minimal tutoring – and it is an interim objective for the conscientious teacher who is flung in at the deep end, having been given nothing in the way of preparation other than a register.

SELF-EXPLORATION

1. **Do you enjoy being a tutor? What aspects of the role do you like? (If you are not a tutor yet, what aspects of the role do you think you will enjoy?)**

2. **What skills do you particularly feel you lack for pastoral work? (Write down the first things that come into your head. Then number them in order of importance.)**

Administration

The most immediate task which a new tutor will have to deal with is administration, and the first administrative job will be marking the register. It may be offensive to suggest that you may not know how to do this, but it is rare for marking the register to be referred to in initial training courses and that is a good reason for considering it here.

It doesn't need a book to point out that if the tutor is not there in the tutor group he won't be able to tell whether the members of the group are there; if he is late he won't know whether his tutees were on time. Moreover, as any member of senior management will tell you, you can't expect your students to be on time if you're habitually late yourself. So the first rule is to make sure that you have given yourself enough time to arrive at the tutor group without feeling harassed.

There are lots of ways of marking a register, and for an experienced teacher almost any of them will work. I have known several tutors who were happy to walk round their group, registering them as they went. But this is for the tutor who is confident of the respect of his tutees, and whose style is particularly relaxed. Teaching above all is a career where you have to make the job suit your personality. That is why it is not easy to give advice about how another teacher should handle a particular situation. In general, however, it is best to start off with a relatively formal regime.

This means that you ask your tutees to sit down and to keep quiet while you call out their names and mark them off in the register. At the beginning of the day this sets the tone appropriately. I used the word 'ask' rather than 'tell' above because the most effective way to teach and gain respect is to offer it yourself. If you are firm about the students being quiet while you carry out this kind of administrative task – that is you don't ignore people who do talk or don't sit down – eventually you will find that you can relax, so that the situation becomes a formal but relaxed one. But relaxed atmospheres have to be worked for, and you should not think you have failed to create the right atmosphere if you feel that you are having to be stricter than you want to be, or than your colleagues appear to be, even for a year or so.

You should not encourage your tutees to think that they can mark the register. After all, attendance – or more particularly, non-attendance – can be a highly confidential matter. Accuracy in a register is also very important, especially considering that prosecutions for non-attendance will start with the register. The register is in fact a legal document. The 1944 Education Act gives the governors of schools the responsibility of keeping an Admissions Register, which will list all students as they enter the school, and an Attendance Register. The Pupils Registration Regulations 1956 lay down that, at the commencement of each morning and afternoon session, the presence or absence of every pupil whose name is entered in the Admissions Register should be marked *in ink* in the Attendance Register. The governors are responsible for its accuracy. However, if you are away and for some reason no-one is able to substitute for you then it may be better if a student is prepared to mark the register in pencil than that no record of attendance at all is kept, though any such entries need to be checked as far as possible when you return.

The actual method of marking the register may vary but the following is a common approach. You should draw a slanting line for 'present', slanting to the right for the morning session and to the left for the afternoon session, so that it is easy to count the number of days, for example, that a student has been present. If the student is absent, put a circle. If the student eventually arrives, put an 'L' inside the circle, so that you can keep a record of 'lates'. If, when the student returns to school after absence, she provides you with a note, put a dot in the centre of each circle; this way, you will be able to see at a glance whether the student has explained her absence. You can put a dot if the parent rings at the outset of the absence.

Other administrative tasks will depend on the school. You may have to read out a daily bulletin of events. You may have to hand out circulars. You may have to get information from your tutees about their ages, the buses they travel on, what they do at lunchtime, and so on. If you know them well, such jobs can be easy. If you don't, as will be the situation during the first day/week/month, then such sessions can be an opportunity to get to know them. Listening to (*not* talking to) a small group who all travel to school on the same bus can be illuminating, not only about your tutees but also about the kinds of situations they have to face each day, and may be an opportunity for learning both for them and for you.

How far you can use such opportunities in a constructive way will depend on the amount of time that you have available. But teachers have to accept that almost everything they do has to be done in far too little time, and to excuse oneself from attempting something worth while on those grounds would mean that one would never attempt anything! Nevertheless, if you want more time, there is no harm in asking if you can have it. So many tutors feel they have too much time with their groups that pastoral team leaders will often be delighted by such a positive attitude.

Doing the administration is not all there is to tutoring. But if you are not going to do much else you must get this right – and at the start you may feel you have little time for anything else. I know tutors whose administration is decidedly sub-standard but whose commitment to their tutees – the care and amount of time and energy they devote to it – makes them excellent tutors.

Tutor periods

Most schools now allot some time – though often not enough – for the tutor to be with his tutor group as well as merely the few minutes given over to registration. What the tutor is expected to do in this time will depend on the school, but there are two main possibilities; some schools practise both while others only expect one. The first is where the tutor may have no particular structure to impose on the group or on the time available, while in the second, the tutor has a topic, methods and organisation which he intends to employ.

UNSTRUCTURED TUTOR TIME

The word 'unstructured' refers to the fact that there is no attempt on the part of the tutor to organise members of the tutor group in any particular way. Thus, they are allowed and encouraged to sit around in whatever groups they wish and talk among themselves. Some may finish off a bit of homework or do some revision, while others may read. But generally, the atmosphere should be that of a relaxed social occasion.

At present the unstructured tutor period is unfashionable, many teachers taking the view that the tutor group ought to be engaged in a planned course of group activities all the time, and that lack of structure generally leads to wasted time. Nevertheless, I want to consider how it should be handled, partly because your school may expect you to handle it and partly because it does have real value when it is approached in a constructive spirit.

The role of the tutor at such times is difficult to define. He is there as an adult supervisor and may intervene if he feels that, for instance, someone is being too noisy. But he can also use this time in a constructive way. His value to the school, after all, is that, quite apart from the skills he may possess in working with young people, the tutor is the person who can know the students best. The unstructured tutor period is an opportunity for him to make this true; in other words, he can use the time to talk with individuals or groups of tutees without having to follow any particular agenda.

This is more demanding for the tutor than it may sound. It requires that he is able to relax with his tutees so that they feel relaxed chatting to him. It requires that he does not put up barriers between himself and his students, so he needs to be able to be himself, not just 'a teacher'. By this I mean that he must not hide behind stock teacher attitudes and responses, must not be automatically judgemental; in other words he must react as far as possible as if he were in conversation with *any* other people. If he is *always* congruent – to use a term from counselling which means that his overt behaviour matches what is going on inside him – then he will find this much easier than if most of the time he is playing the part of a teacher in his dealings with his students.

Teachers who find unstructured time most stressful are those whose relationship with the group or with students in general is based on some kind of pose which involves erecting a barrier between teacher and student. If you feel that you do this, you should ask yourself why you adopt such a role before your students.

You may well decide that it is the fear of losing control. Almost all teachers fear this to a greater or lesser extent, but if the tutor really wants to have a relationship with the students in his group, he needs to make himself vulnerable. It is the teacher's apparent invulnerability which has got in the way in the past, and which lies behind the sense which we all get from time to time that our students think we're not quite human!

The first requirement, therefore, is that the tutor should be himself. Perhaps the most important aspect of this congruence is that he conveys to his students that he is talking to them because he enjoys their company and wants to talk to them, rather than because it is part of his job to talk to them. He is not, in other words, being phoney or patronising them. Most of us are able to sense this kind of duplicity in our dealings with others, and we are usually annoyed by it. It may be that the new tutor will need to spend some time in more formal contact with his tutees before he can chat with them authentically.

I am not suggesting the sort of strategy which involves an attitude of 'coming down to their level'. This expression gives a lot away about the person who uses it, since it suggests – though this is unlikely to be the intention – a contempt for the student. The tutor must above all respect his tutees and respect himself, and an approach which involves an assumption about the teacher's superiority to the student will not be successful – in any context probably – but certainly not in unstructured time.

It is more appropriate that the tutor should approach his tutees in a respectful and friendly way, as with, say, a colleague. After all, at first anyway, your tutees are *not* friends so there is no justification for familiarity. It is a good rule to treat students as you would like to be treated, and if the tutor behaves in a familiar way with his tutees when they are new to him he can be fairly certain that they – or some of them – will treat him in the same way. You may see other tutors who appear to have a familiar relationship with their tutees, but they may have got to know them well enough for this to be acceptable. The rules for behaviour with young people are very similar to those we follow easily enough with adults.

The second requirement is that *all* your tutees feel that you like them, want to talk to them and, care about them, not just *some* of them. Some students gravitate towards the tutor easily, and if you let them will be the only members of the group you get to know. Of course, some won't want to talk to you or will be embarrassed (which may make them seem insolent) or shy. The tutor should make regular attempts to listen to them, however, not – as is easiest – give up on them after the first rebuff.

It is worth keeping a diary of who you have talked to each session. This shouldn't be done openly as it may seem offensive: a head of year/ house who kept a diary of the tutors she spoke to would probably be operating a useful system of consultation, but knowing of it would not make tutors grateful to her!

The third point to consider is your objectives. First, you need to make your tutees feel that you are interested in them and not that you are checking up on them (they have the same fears of appraisal that teachers have!); second, you need to be aware of the pattern of relationships in the group; and third, you need to be monitoring – looking for needs among your tutees.

There is value in using a format, but again it is better if it is not used openly. Going up to a student with a checklist of questions is as offputting as approaching an adult in the same way.

CONVERSATION FORMAT FOR UNSTRUCTURED TIME

1. **How are you getting on in your work at the moment? (Name a few subjects, remembering to include some where you expect the student to be successful – ask head of year/house HOY/H).)**

2. **Who are your friends at the moment?**

3. **How are your parents? How are things at home? (Friendly enquiry. Only follow this up if you get a strong reaction.)**

4 What are you doing with yourself outside school?

All questions can be phrased in a variety of ways to suit you, the student and most of all what you already know of her.

Show your knowledge of the student where you can; eg in Question 4, if you know that she is a keen table-tennis player you can ask about that, and then say; 'Are you doing anything else in your spare time?'

Only push enough to be sure that you've given a genuine opportunity for the student to express worries. Don't dig unless you sense that it is wanted/necessary. It is not advisable to use loaded questions like, 'Have you got any problems at the moment?' Few children/young people will answer yes to that, whatever the circumstances.

The questions mentioned are, of course, intended for use with individuals rather than with groups, but as long as you are careful there is no reason why Questions 1 and 4 should not be done with a group of friends, and may elicit much more forthright responses (though more forthright doesn't necessarily mean more truthful).

There may be occasions when, because of a response in conversation or because you are already aware of a particular situation which needs urgently talking through, it is necessary to spend an unstructured session with one student only. This is not a misuse of the time, though it shouldn't be allowed to happen too often and certainly not too often with the same student. If you think that a particular student needs a lot of individual attention then you should get outside help: someone else with more time should be called upon either to deal with the situation for you or to take over some other part of your workload so that you can devote more time to this student without depriving the other group members of your attention. I shall return to this point when I discuss the tutor's relationship with his head of year/house.

SELF-EXPLORATION
1. Do you enjoy talking with students? What kinds of things do you talk about?

2. Do you tend to do most of the talking or most of the listening?

3. Do you enjoy talking with individual students or with groups more?

4. When have you felt especially uncomfortable in your tutor group? When have you felt especially comfortable? Can you identify what makes you feel comfortable?

STRUCTURED TUTOR TIME

The other kind of tutor period differs less from a lesson than does unstructured time, particularly if you use groupwork in your subject teaching. There are a variety of jargon terms which are used to refer to this kind of activity – the Pastoral Curriculum, Active Tutorial Work (or ATW), Personal and Social Education (PSE), Pro-active Pastoral Care and others. The structured tutorial period is a time in which the tutor, perhaps in negotiation with the members of the group, leads activities, often employing active learning methods and organised in small groups, which are designed to contribute to the supportive function of the group and to assist in the personal and social development of its members.

At present, it is a controversial matter as to the extent to which the tutor should be expected to be responsible for this kind of curricular input. In many schools the tutor is certainly expected to regard it as an important aspect of tutoring, and in some schools it is such activities that the terms 'tutoring' and 'pastoral care' are used to cover, to the virtual exclusion of anything else.

Though such extremes are not desirable, there is no doubt of the benefits of constructive groupwork in creating a sense of identity and unity in the tutor group, nor in the fact that there are some areas of the curriculum for which it is right to exploit the special relationship which we hope will exist between the tutor and his tutees. The whole of Chapter 3 is devoted to this aspect of the work of the tutor, so if this is an urgent need for you, you may want to turn to that chapter now. It is certainly an aspect of creative tutoring, but may also be part of the minimal role in your school, which is why I have included these remarks in this chapter.

Monitoring

Arguably the most important job which a tutor has to do is monitoring the success or otherwise of the student in coping with her life while she is a member of the school. The tutor, under any system and whatever his status in the institution, is one of the people who will see the child most often. The tutor needs to regard knowing the child as well as possible as his first responsibility. In the end, the most stressful aspect of the tutoring role may be that he will be aware that not spotting changes, trends, moods, relationships, and so on in his tutees could mean that problems develop unnecessarily. Also, not spotting capacities, talents and exploitable aspects of character may mean that a person misses opportunities to develop those abilities, and consequently the self-respect which would accompany them, and even perhaps career possibilities.

What is it that we should be monitoring? First and most obviously, we need to monitor our tutees' academic progress.

Some might express surprise that the tutor should be responsible for this: after all, they might say, this is not part of the pastoral role. This view is one which we need to oppose energetically. It is based upon the view that pastoral and academic aspects of school life are entirely separate. In fact, this is far from being the case. Perhaps the most obviously central task of the tutor is to monitor academic progress, since academic development is one of the few agreed objectives of secondary schooling. As well as this, the tutor is the best person to carry it out, since he, unlike the subject teachers or heads of department, has an overview of the whole student. In order to prevent this knee-jerk reaction, we might be advised to talk of curricular rather than academic progress, since what characterises this kind of monitoring is that it concerns those aspects of the student's development which have to do with the formal curriculum. This usage would also have the advantage that it does not apparently exclude the so-called non-academic subjects (though there is far more to the curriculum than what is learned in the classroom – see Chapter 7: 'The Hidden Curriculum', p 144).

The introduction of Records of Achievement will provide a framework into which the monitoring of students' progress can be assimilated, but even before this development takes place it makes sense to learn from its methods and approaches. A basic principle would be that monitoring should take into account not only the viewpoint of the teacher, but also the viewpoint of the student.

Information from the subject teacher will be obtained first through the regular reporting system which virtually all schools operate. The tutor is always involved in this process in that he will collect and collate reports from subject teachers, and will generally write a summary report of his own at the end. Second, there will be times when subject teachers may send a report on a particular student to the tutor, because she has displeased or, hopefully, pleased her. Finally, there will be times when the tutor will wish to solicit reports from staff; this may happen if, for example, a subject teacher reports a deterioration in the standard of a student's work, when the tutor will wish to ascertain whether the problem is limited to one subject or whether the same development has been noted by other staff. This last is one of the particularly important tasks for which the tutor may have responsibility. Traditionally, the head of year/house has tended to take it on with the result that only extreme cases have warranted this treatment. However, it is an aspect of pastoral care which all students should benefit from, and if you practise it – tactfully and with the knowledge of your pastoral head – it is unlikely that anyone will object.

The most straightforward method of obtaining the student's viewpoint is to ask her to write a self-assessment. This is generally most effectively done by following the same kind of format as the teachers' report, and using the official-looking form will tend to encourage to student to take particular care in completing it. Within each subject area, it may help the student if you give her some guidance as to what kinds of comments to make. The format for subject monitoring, outlined below is a suggested approach.

FORMAT FOR SUBJECT MONITORING
1. **In which aspects of this subject do you feel you have done well this term?**

2. **What particular difficulties have you had in this subject? What do you think you might be able to do to improve?**

3. **What have you enjoyed about this subject this term?**

Whenever you receive a report from any source concerning a student in your tutor group you should file it, so that a picture of the student's progress is built up from the regular and *ad hoc* reports. Before you do that, however, you need to discuss the report with the student concerned.

By 'discuss', I mean discuss. There has been a tendency among some well-intentioned teachers to see this kind of interchange as consisting of the teacher explaining to the student why the particular remarks have been made on the report, with the object of – if necessary – convincing her that they are justifiable. While this is preferable to the less well-intentioned teacher who takes the view that it doesn't matter what the student thinks, it still does not accept the validity of the student's view since it assumes that if there is any discrepancy the teacher's view must carry. Such indications of lack of respect are damaging to any attempt to forge the kind of relationship with your tutees which I have referred to and will examine more extensively in Chapter 2. Worse, they prevent the tutor gaining a whole view of the situation, since clearly the student's perception of it is a central aspect.

It is less straightforward in the vast majority of schools to monitor other aspects of students. Schools have long provided some kind of structure for academic monitoring, but there has been little attempt made to provide a similar way of monitoring the extra-curricular, psychological, personal, moral and social development of students.

Recent developments in recording, however, have begun to take this aspect of a student's progress into account. Most models of Records of Achievement provide approaches to this task, usually through some kind of personal record of activities or experience that is kept by the student in consultation with the tutor. If your school is involved in a scheme of this sort, it may be that monitoring personal development will be simpler. If not, a basic tool which you can employ would be to issue your tutees with a notebook in which you can encourage them to keep a record of the activities, visits and achievements in which they are involved outside the classroom and outside school. A diary format is appropriate so that activities can be dated. The notebooks can be kept in the tutor room if this is possible, and can provide tutorial activity perhaps once a week, and a focus for discussion.

As well as the more formal and written monitoring, however, there is a less formal monitoring where the distinction between monitoring and developing your relationship with the tutor group need not be very great. Just as with making good social relations, the first principle is that it is no use monitoring only some students: you have to monitor all the students in the group. It is often easy to monitor the students who naturally please teachers – ie those with easy social skills and those who want to work in the way that the teachers find most acceptable (which varies from teacher to teacher). There are many students who will not be so comfortable with the tutor (or indeed with adults in general) that they will volunteer information about themselves.

In the previous section I suggested a format for regular conversations with members of the tutor group during unsctructured sessions. I shall repeat it below.

CONVERSATION FORMAT (Reprise)
1. **How are you getting on in your work at the moment? (Name a few subjects, remembering to include some where you expect the student to be successful – ask HOY/H.)**

2. **Who are your friends at the moment?**

3. **How are your parents?/How are things at home? (Friendly enquiry. Only follow this up if you get a strong reaction.)**

4. **What are you doing with yourself outside school?**

Clearly, as it stands, this is a fairly crude instrument for monitoring since it can apply to students of all ages equally (which is its value as a conversation prompter since it is easy to memorise). But to monitor effectively it is helpful to aim the questions you ask in such a way as to focus on areas of difficulty – or the reverse – which it is particularly likely that the student will have. To begin with, there are particular questions which you should consider asking members of particular years.

FIRST YEAR
- What do you particularly like about the school?
- What have you not enjoyed so far?

In the first few weeks these kinds of questions in different forms should be asked repeatedly, and as you get to know the strengths and weaknesses of the students you can prompt the less forthcoming student with appropriate ideas.

You will have other sources of information about the student, from parents, from staff who teach her, and so on. Soon you should be able to focus quite accurately on areas of difficulty and success (and the latter is at least as important to discuss with her: teachers have traditionally stressed the former). However, you need to guard against over-confidence in your capacity to know the student. The good tutor should only rarely be surprised by something that a tutee does, because he knows her so well; but all tutors will be taken by surprise sometimes, and all tutors miss things which are happening to their tutees. Since this monitoring task is the crucial job of the tutor, vigilance is the key ability.

Another question you might ask is:

- How are you using your free time in/out of school?

This is a time when some students find social contact difficult. What they find to do in breaks and lunchtimes is an indicator. The answer to the question may also help you to pick out the student who is spending too much or too little time on homework. Outside interests can be a source of self-respect to many students, often particularly to those for whom much of their school experience makes them feel pretty inadequate. Keeping a written record of the achievements of your tutees is a good idea even where such records are not a formal part of the tutor's responsibilities, and to ask about recent successes is a sure way to win a student over.

Apart from these reasons, students may not know about the leisure opportunities which a school has to offer, and may be bored or lonely unnecessarily. You may be able to involve the whole of the group in exploring the variety of ways of passing their free time in school.

SECOND YEAR

The second year is a time when most students have adapted to their new school and are feeling confident about it. Often, it is the year when patterns are set which will decide the student's attitude to work, to friendships, to authority and so on. Some students ease off in the second year: the pressure to impress the new school has gone and examinations are too far away to have any effect. Indeed, some schools seem to do little to discourage the view of the second year as not particularly important. It is therefore appropriate for the tutor to contribute to the impression that this is a critical stage and that the student's attitude in particular is going to be a considerable factor in determining what happens to her later.

Question 1 of the conversation format, with some more detailed supplementaries like:

- What are your favourite subjects at present?

may lead the tutor to signs of disaffection but will also be helpful in revealing information about the abilities of the student.

However, precisely because most youngsters in the second year have settled down, the student who has not done so needs to be identified at an early stage and her particular problems recognised. Particular attention to the friendship question (2) may be revealing.

Using the principle that we have used so far, of asking 'What is happening to this age of student?', think of some more questions which would be appropriate to ask second-year students.

THIRD YEAR

The third-year student needs to be thinking about the future if her option choices are going to be more than a lucky dip, but may not be especially interested in doing so. So add to the questions you direct at her:

- What do you think you may be doing in five years' time?

You may pick up more than career aspirations with this question, of course. The third year, perhaps more than any other stage, is one where the range of maturity is very great, particularly since many of the girls will generally appear to be young women, while the boys may in most cases still look like (and behave like!) children.

Monitoring means making yourself aware of as much as you can with respect to your tutees and their lives but it does not mean prying, and

29

from the third year upwards you may meet more reluctance to share private lives with the tutor. This obviously has to be respected. At the same time, it is not always sensible to be put off by a cold reception. Some young people are embarrassed at being questioned at all, and it has to be done as lightly as possible for this reason. But even the tutee who is embarrassed may actually want to talk to the tutor. It is important to find an opportunity to talk when students who feel this are not with an audience of friends. Even fairly forthcoming young people may feel inhibited when their peers are watching or listening. The result may be that they giggle or catch each other's eyes – and the tutor himself may begin to feel awkward.

Now think what else may affect third-year students particularly: what other two questions might you ask?

FOURTH YEAR
In the fourth year there are many possibilities, but focusing directly on the new and difficult courses which the students have started this year is perhaps the most obvious. This is especially true at the beginning of the year – say up to half-term – but the question needs to be brought back about half-way through the year, when some students become disillusioned with their choices anyway and the tutor may get a string of requests to drop subjects.

A basic question might be:

● Which of your new option choices have been most successful?

It is almost always a good idea to focus on the positive first. There is frequently enough negativity around at this stage without the tutor contributing to it! More importantly, a positive question will encourage the student to consider what she is finding enjoyable and satisfying – which she might otherwise not have done. Nevertheless, you also need to ask the negative question:

● What problems have you got with your new courses?

Note that it is best to ask a question which cannot be answered by yes or no since students then need to give real thought to their answer. Also, monosyllabic answers mean that the tutor has to ask another question. Most students who have no particular problems will say so, though the tutor needs to be aware of the possibility of her manufacturing something to satisfy him.

Now look at other areas which particularly affect the life of the fourth-year student. What about relationships with friends, with parents and with the opposite sex? These are areas where you should be gentle and sensitive in your approach and be prepared to back off, but they are also areas where tutees may be glad to be given the opportunity to talk. What question might you ask which would be friendly, non-threatening and open-ended?

Sometimes students prefer to write when the subject is sensitive: see the section on open-ended aural questionnaires in Chapter 3 (p. 64).

What other areas of conversation might be appropriate to the fourth-year student?

FIFTH YEAR
From the school's point of view it seems that the life of most fifth-year students is dominated by exams and the search for employment, and there is no doubt that for some students and for most students some of the time this is about right. However, fifth-year students will also be affected by their changing perceptions of themselves as they approach adulthood, a fact which the tutor should appreciate rather than seeing his tutees simply as exam-fodder. So obviously the tutor should be asking:

- What plans have you made to cope with the work you've got to do this term?

and:

- What jobs/college places have you applied for so far?

The tutor should also be going over the relationships ground which I referred to in the section on the fourth year. The tutor needs to bear in mind that some students weren't ready for these issues in the fourth year (and indeed that some still won't be in the fifth year). The tutor should be careful to approach the subject in a way that won't make the tutee feel pressured in any way.

For many students this will be their last year in school. What questions might this suggest to you?

I have mainly talked in this section as if all these questions will be asked one-to-one, and indeed that is necessary for some questions and for some students. But there are occasions when the tutor can look for opportunities to ask groups of young people the same kind of questions. Some students are less threatened when they are not being focused on individually, and they are more likely to learn from talking to each other in a way that they will almost certainly not learn when they talk to the tutor – after all, he hasn't got experience of the same situation to draw on.

A discussion of:

● What jobs/college places have you applied for so far?

will often be much more fruitful in encouraging those who haven't applied for anything yet to do so than will teacher exhortations. Douglas Hamblin (1978) rightly stresses the importance of helping the students to see themselves as the main resource for learning of this sort, rather than the teacher.

A lot of monitoring is done by the good tutor much less formally than this all implies – though remember that even the approach I have suggested shouldn't *look* formal. Picking up moods in your tutees, being aware of shifts in relationships, spotting aggression or bullying, noting groups focused on one student – all and many more will arouse your attention. As your tutees learn that you can be trusted they will come to you with their problems or with their worries about their friends. Monitoring your tutor group – like almost everything else in teaching – gets easier as you gain in experience and as the students come to know you.

TAKING MINIMAL ACTION
All the information which you may acquire through the kind of conversation we have been discussing is of course interesting, but monitoring is really a waste of time unless you act on it. As far as minimal tutoring is concerned, acting on it means passing the information on to someone else, who will generally be the head of year/house. You will have to decide what matters enough to be passed on: it should not simply be those things which you think will cause trouble for the school, nor those things which are bad news in some way. You should pass on good news too: information about student achievement is valuable, and if your middle management is willing to make a point of having a word with the student concerned, the benefit for that student will be out of proportion to the amount of effort which you have expended.

To conclude this section, however, I shall give just a glimpse of the follow-up a tutor who wishes to extend the range of his activity and become more creative and more truly responsible for his tutees might take. To do this I shall take an example, that of the answers which might be elicited by the question: 'What problems have you got with your new courses?'

This is an area where follow-up is absolutely essential. The first step is to cross-check with the teacher of the subject which is causing worry. Is the teacher aware of the student's problem? If not, is that because the student's perception is pessimistic; because the teacher is not as aware of her student's difficulties as she might be; or some other reason? How far is the solution to the problem within the student's own power?

A further follow-up which needs to be considered is to see if other subject teachers have noticed similar problems with this student: the teacher may only be aware of not keeping up with notetaking in physics, but it may have been spotted as a problem in history as well. This is also a time when the tutor should be talking to the head of year/house who may have information about the student's past performance which is relevant. She needs to be informed anyway, as her job will at the very least involve *co-ordinating* the monitoring and she needs to know what monitoring the tutor has done and what information has emerged.

So: ask the student a question; elicit an answer; follow-up with a relevant subject teacher; follow-up with other subject teachers; and discuss with HOY/H.

SELF-EXPLORATION

1. What questions could you be asked which would reveal your successes this year? What about your difficulties?

2. What questions would you object to being asked?

3. What do you think are the implications for your students of your answers here?

Authority within the tutor group

New teachers almost invariably find that there are some students who they dislike. Usually they are students who threaten the teacher's authority and therefore self-respect. Authority in this context is difficult to define, but in general if a teacher has authority he will be able to induce students to co-operate with him. There are probably as many ways of having authority as there are personalities and the first principle is to find out about yourself so as to assess how you can use your personality so that you have the authority that you need.

Traditionally, teachers have used fear to coerce students to co-operate. This is now much less effective than it was, for a number of reasons. First, society now employs fear very little outside the school context and though there is certainly ambivalence in society's attitude towards that approach to discipline, few find it acceptable when it is directed towards themselves or their families and friends. Parents are much less ready to accept summary justice meted out to their offspring by teachers. Connected with this change is the disappearance in Britain of corporal punishment as a method of control in schools. Fear requires punishment and the punishment needs to be sufficiently unpleasant to arouse it. It is necessary in order to create a climate of fear to have a hierarchy of punishment, the final resort of which should be universally feared. Exclusion, which is the ultimate sanction in most local authorities, is to be feared if it is accompanied by shame, but though this is certainly the case in many families it is not in some. It may have the effect of interfering with the examination prospects of the student, but the effectiveness of that in arousing fear depends on the prospects of the particular student. Finally, many teachers are themselves opposed to disciplinary approaches which depend on fear.

Apart from such pragmatic arguments, it does seem to me that if schools are to provide a training ground in which students can learn how to operate in society, discipline which is based on coercion and violence is an inappropriate preparation. What is needed is for the school to develop in its students a respect for the rights of other people and a consequent self-discipline, since that is what is needed in society.

It is therefore better to base one's authority upon something other than fear. It is not unduly informative to say that the teacher needs to be respected since it is possible to be respected for all kinds of reasons. It is, however, helpful to see being liked as a method of control, as long as being liked does not conflict with being respected.

In Chapter 5 I outline the results of the research into counselling styles undertaken by Truax and Carkhuff (1967) and into teaching styles by Aspy and Roebuck (1977). The latter work, entitled *Kids Don't Learn from People They Don't Like*, angles its findings specifically towards the teacher, but the qualities it identifies as leading to children liking them are substantially the same as those which result in more effective counselling.

To put it straightforwardly, if they are to like a teacher students need to feel, first, that he understands what it feels like to be a student in that institution; second, that the face he presents to them is a genuine one, not a mask put on for the purpose of self-protection; and finally, that he really likes them and that that liking is not conditional upon their behaving in some particular way.

The problem for the new tutor, however, is often that a student who feels the need to test the boundaries which the tutor is prepared to tolerate may arouse fear in the tutor, so that he comes to dislike her. He may also resort to hiding behind the authority which the role of the teacher itself gives him, so that he is not able to be himself, and is too concerned about his own preservation to be able to empathise with the student.

The important thing to do is to separate the individual from the group. I mean this both in a conceptual and a physical sense. First, it is essential to resist the temptation to impose on the group as a whole the characteristics of the individual student who is causing the problem; to think, in other words, that the whole group is a problem. The temptation is strong because for the tutor it is this student who, if he is not careful, will dominate his image of the group. But there are a number of other students in the group at least some of whom will be well-disposed towards the tutor, and it is unfair and damaging to their interests to imagine that they are not.

Second, the student who is causing the problem needs to be *physically* separated from the group before specific action is taken. If you try to deal with her in the group, the whole group will be involved, will feel that they are implicated and may very well resent it. They will then provide you and the 'problem student' with an audience, which will mean that, because neither of you will be able to lose face, the situation will develop a competitive edge. In that case, if you win she may very well never forgive you – and losing publicly will create further problems with the uncommitted members of the group, who may be encouraged to take you on themselves. Confrontation is a bad idea, but it is especially unfortunate in public.

In private, you need to make it clear where you draw the lines of acceptable behaviour and to explain clearly and quietly how you perceive her to have crossed them. You then need to give her an opportunity to put her side, and you must listen and not interrupt. You now have a dialogue. If you are honest and genuine in the reasons you give for finding her behaviour unacceptable, most students will perceive the justice of what you say – assuming that you are in the right. If you are not in the right, when you try to be honest, this too will be apparent, and it is a lot easier to admit to being in the wrong one-to-one than in front of a group.

There is no need to shout, to talk over the student or to bully her. The tutor needs to display courtesy even when he is reprimanding the student.

What you must not do is ignore behaviour which you find intolerable.

In the end, your resentment or fear or anger will reach the point where you do react, and because it is without warning it may well be perceived as an overreaction, even by the neutrals in the group.

Spelling out the rules by which you intend to run the group – which will vary according to what you want them to do – will often avoid this kind of situation arising, as long as you pick up deviators immediately. Remember that if you have been allowing them to talk for an activity and then want them to be quiet this may have to be made clear: the rules have changed. Once you have changed the rules, don't confuse the group by switching back to the old rules without making it very clear what you are doing. It is often ambiguity as to precisely where the boundaries of acceptable behaviour lie that causes so-called disruptive behaviour.

Authority does not mean being 'tough'. That is one method, and one which is less acceptable now than it used to be. It means communicating a sense that you are in charge, that you know what you are doing and what you expect of your class. Partly it is confidence, which grows with experience. But partly it is simply that you *do* know what you expect of them.

SELF-EXPLORATION
1. In what situations do other adults do as you ask them to?

2. How do you feel when you give students an instruction which is not obeyed? What do you do about it? Does that strategy work? What other strategies could you try?

3. What qualities have you got which mean that your group may benefit from doing what you ask them to do? How will their interests be damaged if they don't? (be honest).

4. Do you want to be an effective disciplinarian? Give reasons for your answer.

Chapter 2

Tutor Ascendancy and Tutoring Relationships

Tutor ascendancy

In the Introduction, I briefly defined the term 'tutor ascendant'. In this chapter I shall explain the term in more detail, and then consider the implications which an ascendant role for the tutor has for the relationships which the tutor has to develop with the various people with whom he works.

Tutor ascendancy involves the notion that the tutor is fully responsible for the pastoral care of his tutor group, and that he initiates most action which is taken by the school. The ascendant tutor is to be regarded as responsible for his tutees, in the sense that they are wholly in his care and also in the sense that he will feel that he can share in the credit or otherwise which is due to them.

Douglas Hamblin argues that this notion – of the tutor as responsible for his tutees – is threatening to the tutor, who regards it as implying that he will be blamed for the misdemeanours of his tutees. This seems to me to be a particularly negative view, akin to saying that a parent's responsibility involves centrally that she will be blamed for her child's misdemeanours. A conscientious parent no doubt does feel responsible for what her offspring does – and a conscientious tutor will too – but just as there is a lot more to parenting than this, so there is a lot more to tutoring than just getting blamed when something goes wrong.

The same might also be said of any responsibility which a person has; clearly, responsibility can create apprehension, but it also leads to greater job satisfaction when the responsibility is acquitted successfully. This seems to me to be particularly true with regard to tutoring, where the sense of only being able to cope with routine administration and 'first base contact' (Culshaw and Eustance, 1983) and where the moment things get interesting a head of year or house comes along and whips it away, is particularly damaging to teacher morale. To regard teachers as professionals, and competent and sensitive at that, is a constructive move towards better morale in the teaching profession.

Some teachers argue that tutors sometimes make gaffes with parents, and cause damage to relationships. I don't doubt that such things happen, but heads of year – also deputy heads and even heads – have been known to make similar mistakes. It is an argument for better (some!) training, not for allowing a particularly rewarding part of the teacher's job to be hived off to a few people.

A further objection which is often raised is that tutors don't want to take on any more work than they already have. There are various concerns behind this. Tutors are concerned that they shouldn't be expected to take on more work without being given appropriate time in which to do it. Nor should they. A school which is genuinely committed to the notion of the ascendant tutor must show that commitment in giving the tutor pastoral time in which to fulfil that role.

It is also argued that teachers shouldn't be expected to take on tasks which they are not competent to do – for which they haven't had training. Part of this is unwarranted modesty. Most teachers are capable of a range of flexible and sensitive relationships – and prove that they are in their everyday teaching. Such qualities make them admirably suited to be tutors. But certainly a school which is asking tutors to be ascendant needs to offer training, partly as a way of helping them to recognise their own competences and exploit them.

However, both the above arguments are often produced not by the tutors themselves, many of whom are frequently interested in extending their role beyond the menial tasks of register-marking, list-making, etc, but by heads of year/house. Pastoral heads have an ulterior motive for arguing against an ascendant role for their tutors. The fact is that they enjoy the role they have, enjoy operating one-to-one with students. This is why they went into pastoral middle management in the first place. They are therefore suspicious of anything which seems to threaten their monopoly of this kind of work. They also fear that maybe there will be no role for them if tutors do all the pastoral work. These concerns are understandable, though they should be put aside if the tutor ascendant will provide better pastoral care. Neither would I accept that the pastoral head becomes redundant in a tutor ascendant school: what happens is that she takes on a modified – but no less valuable or rewarding – role. I shall examine what that might be later in this chapter.

The tutor-tutee relationship

To say that the tutor is responsible for his tutees is to say that he is to be regarded as being intimately involved in every aspect of the student's (school) life. I parenthesise the word 'school' on the grounds that the question of whether the student's life out of school is within the sphere of activity of the tutor is extremely controversial. This is an issue which I shall consider below (pp 45–6). For now, I shall simply remark that many students are not able to compartmentalise the different areas of their lives – though there are certainly some who can and for whom this capacity is a blessing since it enables them to find in school a stable focus in what may be an otherwise chaotic or insecure existence. For the majority of students, however, what happens at home will have an impact on what happens at school, and the home life is therefore of concern to the tutor.

It is possible to characterise the tutor-tutee relationship in general terms by saying that the tutor is personally affected by anything that matters to the tutees, and that, as I remarked in Chapter 1, he is rarely taken by surprise by a member of the group, so well does he know them. This is of course the ideal. In practice, there will be students in the group with whom the tutor, despite his best endeavours, is less involved, and there are clearly occasions on which he will be taken aback by some unpredicted behaviour by a tutee. Nevertheless, the ideal does express the kind of relationship which is to be striven for.

Clearly, the precise relationship which the tutee is able to have with her tutor will depend on the personalities of the two people concerned. There is, however, a further factor: the climate of the school. There are still schools which discourage close relationships between staff and students, and expect their staff to maintain the gulf which has traditionally existed. In such schools, pastoral care is unequivocally subversive, and indeed is certainly perceived as such.

The only way in which the aspiring ascendant tutor can affect such a regime is to go his own way, and in so doing to incur the displeasure of senior management. In almost all schools there are staff who will find the tutor who has a close accepting relationship with students threatening. Indeed in a sense they are right to do so since once this kind of relationship becomes commonly accepted it becomes much more difficult for other staff to maintain what might be called the authoritarian stance.

Perceived from the point of view of the kind of tutor I am advocating, there are advantages in being in either kind of school. Where the tutor is supported by a pastorally orientated ethos, clearly students more readily accept, and expect to have, close relationships with staff. Also, and perhaps even more important, using non-authoritarian methods of control is going to be much more easily understood and supported when those methods are usual than when they are the exception. On the other hand, students who need such a relationship but who are members of schools where this approach is rare may have a greater appreciation for what the tutor is offering, so there are compensations!

So what kind of relationship am I advocating? First, I don't think it is quite an equal relationship. If the tutor is to be of use, the tutee has got to feel that he is in touch with the school authorities – that he is able to do something practical to help when this is needed. Also, the tutor has to have the authority within the group to ensure that everyone in the group gets, as it were, a fair crack of the whip. The tutor who is perceived to be capable of being dominated by his tutees is of less use to them.

Nevertheless, the tutoring relationship need not be the same as that the teacher has with the same students in his lessons (though it may be). Teachers should always be approachable, but approachability like other qualities has its degrees, and the tutor needs to be very approachable indeed. I like to characterise the tutor-tutee relationship as that of an elder sibling, an accepting parent or a 'friend on the staff'. Whether it is precisely one of these, and which one, will depend on the tutor concerned, and maybe the tutee concerned too.

Whichever it is, what we are looking for is someone who has most of the following qualities. First, he needs to be able to feel entirely *relaxed* with his tutees, as a group and individually. If he is not then his tutees will not feel relaxed with him. Secondly, he must not have the attitude that everything he says is incapable of improvement: he must be prepared to admit he is wrong, be open to negotiation and listen – genuinely expecting to learn – to his tutees. He must *respect* his tutees, in other words, as human beings; respect their rights, their opinions, their feelings and their perceptions of their own experiences.

Furthermore, he must be entirely *honest* both with himself and with the members of his tutor group. He should expect the same of his tutees as this openness can only work when it is two-way. I do not pretend that this is easy: there are certainly times when there will be conflicts – for instance, between this requirement and the tutor's duties to his colleagues – but such a relationship is an aim to be striven for. If the tutor cannot tell the whole truth about some situation, then he must say that he can't and give, if possible, the real reason why he can't.

He must be *accepting* in his relationship with his tutees. While a tutee should be concerned about his opinion of her actions, she must never feel that she will be rejected if he finds out what she has done. Part of her confidence will arise from the fact that she knows that he will distinguish between the agent who commits the act (whatever it is) and the act itself. If he feels therefore that a tutee has acted wrongly, the tutor must therefore be able to put across his disapproval of the act without transferring that disapproval to the tutee. The tutor must always be working to build or enhance the tutee's positive self-image. Tutees must see one of the roles of their tutor as supporting them when they are in conflict with school authority. (A member of my House recently wrote, '... and my tutor gets tired of having to stick up for me when I get into trouble', which suggests that her tutor was fulfilling that role.)

Part of the tutee's confidence, however, will arise out of the fact that she knows her tutor cares and that he is *disinterestedly concerned* for her well-being. It is the comparative lack of emotional involvement which gives the tutor opportunities which the parent is rarely fortunate enough to have. For while the tutor should certainly care, he is not involved in his tutees' lives, and can be calmer in his reaction to undesired behaviour than most parents can manage to be. The balance between care and detachment will vary, and I have known excellent tutors who were frankly not very detached at all; I have not known any good tutors who did not care at all, however.

SELF-EXPLORATION
Consider the following situations. Now write out the conversation which you would have with the tutees concerned.

1. You walk into your tutor base. No-one seems to notice. They just carry on talking among themselves.

2. You forget to read out the daily notices, and a second-year girl points it out to you.

3. Senior management ask you to ensure that none of your tutor group have brought cigarettes into school.

4. A member of your group tells you that she has stolen money from her mother's handbag.

5. You find a girl and boy in your group cuddling during the lunch-hour in your tutor base.

6. A fifth-year tutee whispers your nickname just loudly enough for you to hear as you pass him.

7. You have been asked by your head of year/house to collect money for charity. At the end of the collection, you find that the amount you have is far less than you think other tutor groups will have collected.

Now think about or discuss with a colleague whether your reactions were (a) the ones you would really give, or (b) the ones you would like to give, or (c) both.

The tutor-parent relationship

The parent of the secondary school student is a crucial resource to the school. Children need to be given the same messages by all the people who have responsibility for them if they are to feel secure and if their behaviour is to be stable. I would like to see some research on this, but my impression is that there is a correlation between deviant behaviour in young people and dissonance in parental attitudes, and indeed it makes sense that the child who receives a set of expectations from one parent which are constantly undermined by the other will not grow up with a clear set of values.

The same seems to be the case in school-parent relationships. Where parents constantly undermine the values of the school (or indeed – and the parents' perception is as valid as the school's – vice versa), the child's behaviour with regard to any aspect of his school life where that dissonance occurs is likely to lack stability.

It is vital then for the tutor to know and understand what his tutee's parents are saying to her at home, particularly with regard to school work, behaviour at school and so on. To give a particularly common example, the student who takes homework back to a home where homework is sneered at or disapproved of is unlikely to execute it particularly well. Equally, a student whose parents have generally enforced their will by recourse to physical punishment may not immediately respect authority which is not supported physically.

Understanding the parents' attitudes to the school, to bringing up children, their aspirations with regard to their children's future and so on, is vital if the tutor is to understand his tutees. Clearly, the school cannot adapt its policies to fit each family, but the tutor can bear the parents' views in mind. It can make its policies clear to them, and this is another task which a tutor should set himself. Communication must therefore be two-way.

The job of the tutor then is, first, to make it *easy* for the parent to communicate with him; second, to make it *worth while* for the parent to communicate with him; and third, both to communicate to the parent the school's expectations and policies, as they affect her children, and give frequent *feedback* about her child's progress and development in school.

The last of these is what schools have done traditionally anyway, but this does not mean that it has been done well. Report writing by schools is sometimes a discredit to the teaching profession, as a glance at the NACRO paper 'School Reports in the Juvenile Court' (NACRO Working Group, 1984) will confirm. There are two kinds of error and they represent two opposed philosophies, though paradoxically it is possible to find them coexisting in the same school sometimes. The first, and much the more serious, is where the report is used to express hostility towards or even wreak vengence on the student. This sounds perhaps overdramatic, but since the school report can be extremely influential in some contexts, it may not be.

For instance, at a relatively trivial level is the teacher who wants to write a report on a student who she has been unable to handle in her lessons, so that she can tell the student's parents who will then be angry at their offspring. This may seem fair enough. However, the teacher who employs the same philosophical approach to writing job references may take the line that 'since Diane has been a nuisance to me, I'm damned if I shall be any help to her', and thereby possibily sabotage her chances of a particular job. Or worse, in the context of the court report, thoughtlessly vindictive remarks could influence a magistrate to deal more harshly than the offence warrants when sentencing.

The opposite error is to make such an effort to write only positive remarks on reports that the parents, for whom the report may be virtually the only medium they have through which to judge the progress of their child, are misled. This kind of report writing is the source of the perennial teacher nightmare of the irate parent complaining about her child's examination results which are so much below expectations – and who can blame her when she has been given no realistic account of what she should expect? Such report writing is also unfair to the conscientious student who may be given a similar report to that of a student who is less so.

If the same approach is adopted when writing job references, it won't be long before the larger employers cease to pay much attention at all to references from that school or that teacher, which again penalises the candidate who deserves a strong reference.

Good report writing should be clear and comprehensible to the parent (who is not familiar with the workings of the school or with educational jargon); at the same time it should be respectful of the student and appreciative of her good qualities. Chapter 6 deals in detail with the question of recording and reporting.

A principle which I recommend particularly in regard to letters to parents, but which is also applicable to reports, is that of the 'bad news sandwich', where any unfavourable criticism is placed carefully in the middle of the letter, with kinder remarks at the beginning and end. This way the reader (the parent, for instance) will begin the letter sympathetically, prepared to listen to what comes next, take in the middle where the 'bad news' is and finish the letter without resentment, and therefore be much more likely to co-operate with whatever the tutor requests.

Even so, however good a letter may be the tutor needs to consider whether some other form of communication might be more effective. Sometimes, the value of a personal telephone call where the tone of voice can ameliorate the content, or even more of the face-to-face contact, will make the extra effort or time taken well worth while.

Parents vary in their attitude to receiving a visit to the home from a teacher. It is important to remember that it may be seen as threatening, particularly if the parents feel that the tutor only visits to complain. But if the tutor can convey a positive spirit towards the student, parents are often appreciative of the effort which the tutor is making. Some schools have developed this principle to the point where all tutors make home visits as a matter of policy early on in the students' school lives, so that later contacts are seen as part of a continuous relationship.

Sometimes, of course, the parent herself may instigate a contact. It is an opportunity for the tutor if the parent spontaneously visits the school. The general impact which the school has on visitors is very important, but it is not, as is often thought, that parents want to see total silence and regimentation. What is most important is that the parents feel welcome on the premises. The school has to convey the impression to any parent that she is not regarded as a threat: her unexpected arrival will not be greeted with embarrassment nor will she be rapidly ushered from one place to another, as if there are parts of the school which are best kept under wraps. I do not think that we need to worry about a parent seeing the occasional less harmonious scene: rumours of life in secondary schools are rife and are such that the reality is certain to be an improvement! The parent should be received as though her arrival is a pleasant surprise. If the visit is unexpected and the tutor is busy, the parent should be asked to wait while the task is completed; if he is teaching, the parent might be taken to the lesson – why not? Under no circumstances must the parent be made to feel that their presence is unwanted.

The individual tutor cannot decide this policy for the school as a whole, but he may be able to decide it for the parents of his own tutees. This looks decidedly like subversion to some staff, but they may be surprised by the positive results. If you can do so, sound out other members of staff about this policy. I suggest three possible groups: the head, your pastoral head and staff whom you think may agree with you.

If you can get the support of the head, it is probably only a matter of time before it is school policy; the pastoral head's support may mean that she will carry the can if anybody objects. The best way to implement change is to work through a pressure group of like-minded individuals.

Whatever support you can get for inviting parents to come in to see you when they like, remember that other staff will resent it if they are involved unwillingly. Under no circumstances should you allow a parent to visit another member of staff unexpectedly unless you prime that colleague first: even the most co-operative colleague may resent interruption in the middle of classroom activity.

Parents will only be encouraged to make such visits if they feel they are going to get something out of them. Obviously, if the visit is unexpected it may not be possible to give the parent all the information she requires immediately, but she must be made to feel that her visit has made things happen. Above all, if the tutor says that he will take some action – ring her back when he has the information, for example – then he must make sure he does so. Taking no action after a parent has visited the school is the surest way of making sure that she never visits again.

If you want to get full parental support, the object of the tutor-parent relationship should be *no secrets on either side*. The problem with this is that such a requirement can sometimes conflict with the relationship the tutor wants to have with his tutee. It may be that the tutee would regard a close relationship between her tutor and her parent as a threat, and certainly as a reason to be fairly cautious about what she tells her tutor. There is no easy answer to this. The only rule of thumb is that the tutor's overall concern is for the student, and the purpose of the close relationship with the parent is to help the student. If the tutor perceives that a close relationship with her parent is going to have a damaging effect upon the interests of the student then it may be that he would be justified in keeping some of what he is told to himself. This is highly controversial – and rightly so, since it questions one of the more obvious parental rights – and the tutor will have to decide his own position. Whatever his view, however, the tutee should never be put in the position of believing that she is talking in confidence when in fact she is not. Nor, of course, should the parent – or anyone else for that matter.

There are people – teachers, parents and students – who feel strongly that it is not the place of the teacher, whatever her role, to involve herself in the home life of other people's children. I have already suggested that this is a difficult view to sustain if what is happening at home is affecting work, social capacity, behaviour, happiness or whatever, at school. It seems to me that if you care about someone, as a tutor may for his tutees, you don't stop caring about them to order. Indeed, for a tutor to show that he does care about them beyond the realms of classroom performance may be invaluable in his relationship with the student, and indeed with her parents.

Nevertheless, we have to respect privacy, and just occasionally this is what parents and students want. We have to be available to be used in whatever way we are needed, but if either the student or her parents do not wish to involve us then it is not part of our job to insist. We may, of course, find situations in which one party but not the other wishes us to be involved. The situation where parents want us to work with them but the student would prefer us to keep out is familiar to anyone who has a disciplinary role in schools (which is virtually all teachers), but the opposite case, where the parent resents the tutor's interference but the student is actually valuing – even asking for – her tutor's help, is also a frequent occurrence. In such cases we need to keep in mind our main function – the care of the student – and to act in the case of conflict in her interests.

SELF-EXPLORATION
Consider the following situations. What would you do?

1. A parent rings you up and asks you to talk to her daughter who, she says is being sulky and unco-operative at home.

2. A boy in your tutor group comes to you and asks if he can talk to you in confidence. He says he won't tell you anything until you give him that assurance.

3. A parent walks into your lesson while you are teaching and starts talking to you about a problem concerned with his son.

Relationships with other staff

WITH THE PASTORAL HEAD
It may be that you are working in a school where the pastoral head is unwilling to allow you the kind of ascendancy which I have been advocating. If this is the case, you will need to employ tact and patience if you hope to extend the tutor's role beyond menial tasks such as marking the register and making lists. Advice relating to this kind of situation can be found in Chapter 7.

If you are fortunate enough to be working in a school where the pastoral middle management are happy to give the tutor whatever scope he wants, then the role of the head of year/house will be rather different

– at least with respect to the tutor – than that which she has traditionally had. It is worth while at this point exploring briefly what this role will be.

First, the pastoral head or leader will co-ordinate the pastoral activities going on in her year/house/section. She will keep in close touch with all her tutors so that she knows what their main concerns are at any one time; she will oversee regular record keeping; she will clarify policy within her section; and she will ensure that no tutor group is being deprived by inadequate tutoring and will act as a safety net if she discovers that it is.

Second, she will be available as a consultant. Ideally, she will have been trained in counselling and in management, but even if she is not she will be an experienced teacher and as such a resource of advice on how to handle situations which may be new to the tutor. She ought to be making time to provide this facility regularly and frequently for each of her tutors, but especially for those who are new to the job.

Third, she should be available to offer support to the tutor. There are times when a relationship with a particular tutee may not be satisfactory, and the pastoral head needs to be able to act as an intermediary in such circumstances. Indeed, in the first couple of years with a new tutor group, the tutor may need a lot of support in developing a constructive relationship with the group as a whole, and this is something which the pastoral head should be aware of and assisting with. This is likely to be the case if the group is a senior one, where there may be resentments about losing the previous incumbent which may (unfairly) be focused on the new tutor. It will also happen with the older members of vertical tutor groups.

There may be times, too, when tutors will need support in dealing with other staff. The staff referral is a particularly common and difficult problem for the new tutor and I will deal with it in detail in the next section, but some of these occasions will benefit from the intervention of a senior member of staff on the tutor's side.

Fourth, the pastoral head should function as a staff counsellor, being responsible for the welfare and development of her tutors. She should no more regard the staff's private life as irrelevant to their professional one than she does that of her students, though the same qualifications have to be made about unwanted interference in the private affairs of tutors that I have made with respect to the tutees.

Finally, and perhaps most important of all, she should be a trainer. Part of this function is fulfilled by the support and consultancy which she provides. But as well as this a good school will make time for in-house training of a more formal kind by pastoral middle and senior management.

We have not, of course, reached the point where I can expect many tutors reading this book to recognise the above model as the one which is to be found in their own schools. Nevertheless, many pastoral heads now accept that it is a desirable end to be working towards – and indeed will value the tutor who wants to be ascendant.

SELF-EXPLORATION
Consider the following situations. What would you do? How would you feel?

1. Your pastoral head shows you a court report which she has written on one of your tutees. You disagree with some of the comments on his attitude and behaviour.

2. A girl from your tutor group comes to see you. She wants to talk to you about the difficulties she is having in relating to her parents at present. Your pastoral head regards all student counselling as his job, but the girl doesn't want to talk to him.

3. Your pastoral head asks you to discipline a student in your group for an offence in her lesson.

4. Your pastoral head wishes to interview one of your tutees and refuses to tell you what it is about.

HANDLING REFERRALS FROM OTHER STAFF
The relationship between the tutor and other staff needs to be one of equality where no one teacher is seen as having a monopoly of authority or competence. It should be one in which all staff offer and accept support from a colleague when the situation demands, and where there is no stigma attached to seeking help or advice.

The tutor (and almost all staff will be tutors), by virtue of the close and ongoing relationship which he has with the members of his group, will be a source of valuable information for his colleagues. Also, the tutor may be able to offer support in cases of conflict. It will be useful to explore this kind of referral to the tutor in detail, since through it relationships with both staff and students can be characterised.

Increasingly in schools the tutor is expected to take referrals – in practice, mostly complaints about behaviour – from other staff about students in his tutor group. This is entirely in tune with the role of the tutor which this book advocates, but it can be one of the less congenial aspects of the job, and sometimes one of the least rewarding – though this is not necessarily the case.

To receive a referral from another member of staff should not be seen as in any way threatening: it is after all part of that member of staff's recognition that you have a particular relationship with the student concerned which enables you to support your colleague. There are occasionally teachers who will refer maliciously – to test a tutor's competence, perhaps expecting to complain afterwards when the student's behaviour is not improved. However, such cases are rare and it is not in anyone's interest to assume that a referral is of this sort.

First, it is beneficial to consider what advantages you have as the student's tutor, which the referer does not have. It is probable that you have a much greater knowledge of the student's background. You may have built up a trusting relationship with her parents (you should certainly be working towards this end). You will know what incidents there have been previously, which other members of staff have made similar complaints, which teachers the student trusts and whether there is any common strand which can be identified in the behaviour concerned. If you are very lucky (or skilled), the student may actually feel any or all of a range of positive attitudes towards you. She may like you, trust you, be grateful to you, want to please you or perhaps just not dislike you as much as she does the other teacher! There may have been previous complaints of the same sort and you have learnt how best to approach this particular student.

Secondly, you need to be aware of your own agenda, your objectives in the situation or what you have in mind when you approach the student. Are you intending to help the student? Or is your main aim to help your colleague or show solidarity with her? Or do you have in your agenda a general aim of order and discipline within the school? Whatever your agenda includes, you should not start out thinking you are helping the student if that is not what you are doing. If you do, the student will get the message from your behaviour that you are saying one thing and thinking something different. Also, if you think you are trying to help her, when she reacts with resentment (which she may), you will respond resentfully, thinking 'How dare she react like that when I'm trying to help her!'

There is actually nothing wrong in having a mixed agenda as long as you are clear what is contained in the mixture. You should aim to support your tutee since this is part of your role as her tutor: it is unlikely that anyone else will if you don't. You should also aim to support your colleague, because mutual support between teachers is important: at the most pragmatic, you may need her help with one of her tutees one day!

You will probably also have a concern for some degree of order in the school in general.

None of these duties is inalienable, however. Sometimes, the student's rights must come before those of a mere institution. We cannot ever assume that a teacher, merely because she is a teacher – or, worse, merely because she is an adult — is necessarily in the right. The tutor needs to be open-minded enough to believe that even teachers are wrong sometimes. After all, all human beings make mistakes and it is not unprofessional to include your colleagues among the ranks of human beings! However, it is unprofessional to believe that when a student and a teacher disagree the student will always be the one who is wrong.

Equally, though, your tutee may be in the wrong. It is possible when you work closely with a student to build up a relationship with her where you actually do not see the kind of insupportable behaviour which your colleagues are confronting constantly. Realistically, too, the fact that it is very good for morale to get into that kind of relationship means that the tutor can sometimes be manipulated by a student so that he finds the horror stories which his colleagues tell about her impossible to credit.

The first thing you should do when you have received a complaint about a tutee is to tell her what you have been told. You should do this factually, being careful not to give the impression that you either believe the complaint before you have heard her side, nor that you only need to hear a word from the student to reject the complaint completely. The former will cause resentment, even if the complaint is justified; the latter will encourage the student to attempt to manipulate you. You also need to avoid sounding punitive at this stage. On the whole, if students have learnt that you are fair, that they will get what they deserve and that you will listen to their side, most will tell you the truth. If the student admits the offence then you can move on to the next stage, your task being made infinitely easier. If she does not, the situation becomes a matter of judgement; this must be based partly on your experience both of young people in general and also of this student in particular. The first thing to do is to establish points of disagreement. We have to work on the assumption initially that no-one is lying, and that where the accounts differ it is a difference of perception. The aim here is to investigate how close the student is prepared to come to the account of the incident given by the referer.

Often, during this process, it will suddenly become clear what actually took place: you can understand why the teacher was so worried by the student's behaviour, and you can also understand what it was that made the student behave as she did. You can check with the student if your interpretation of the incident is correct, and then it becomes a matter of mediating between student and teacher, so that each understands as far as possible the attitude of the other. The student may still have been in the wrong, and action of some sort may need to be taken, but you can at least communicate to her that you understand why she acted as she did. Under such circumstances, it is usually possible to support your colleague, maintain good order and yet at the same time support your tutee so that the relationship between you and her is not damaged.

At the worst, the account of the incident provided by the student differs from that of the teacher in some significant respect. The word 'significant' needs to be stressed: it is pointless to spend time trying to get accounts to cohere when the significant aspects are not being questioned. It is, for instance, of little significance what precisely was said once the level of rudeness is established. But there are cases where the student stands by an account which radically alters the way in which the incident can be viewed. Sometimes, it may cast the teacher in an unfavourable light. For instance, a teacher may have reported a student to you for swearing at her. The student, however, responds that she only swore at the teacher when she made an insulting and insensitive remark to her. It may not justify the student's behaviour but it alters the way a fair-minded and neutral person will view what has happened. It is even harder when the student is accused of an action which she says never occurred at all; for example, she herself said nothing so it must have been someone else.

In such a case, you have to ask yourself some important questions, the answers to which may not be conclusive but will be indicators. Has the student to your knowledge lied before to get out of trouble? Is the behaviour described similar to how she has behaved before? Is the teacher someone who can generally be relied upon not to jump to conclusions or overreact? Is the class likely to have been orderly at the time, or might it have been a situation in which misattribution could easily occur?

Also, with experience comes some capacity to tell when a student is lying. It is not just the classic of not being able to look you in the eye: students who wish to manipulate teachers often know that one as well as we do, so they sometimes give themselves away by brazenly staring into the teacher's face. But there always are students who can lie so convincingly that the most perceptive teacher will be unable to tell. It is much more effective to work hard to create an environment in which lying plays little part. Students lie most when they perceive the context to be a competition between staff and students. So it is not only that they should trust you to be fair, they should also feel that it is not a game: it is a serious business which is taking up time which could be put to better use. (This is one of the reasons for as far as possible seeing that school rules are justified – that they are not just *capable* of justification, but are really there for the purpose which is claimed for them. This may not be within your power to decide, though as a member of the staff you may be able to play your part.)

In the last resort, you may have to bring the student and the member of staff together. You should avoid doing this if at all possible if the teacher concerned is likely to view it as a questioning of her word. If you are going to do it, you should warn the member of staff beforehand; you should discuss with the student how she is going to handle the situation and rehearse any foreseeable difficulties; and you should be present as well. Again, you need to be clear what your agenda is: if it is a matter of proving to the student that she did do what she is accused of you should be aware of that, and should probably be honest with the student that that is why the meeting is taking place.

This kind of meeting works best when you simply want to bring two parties together to discuss what has happened and try to come to some kind of peace or truce. It is therefore worth considering in circumstances where there is no disagreement about what happened. The frank and open discussion can result in real understanding if both parties go into it prepared to see the other point of view, and can be far more effective than punishment. It is also very effective modelling for the student of the peaceful resolution of conflict through discussion and mediation – education in action!

Which brings me to the question of what action you take once you have established that the student was in the wrong. There is no reason to suppose that punishment will necessarily improve the person on whom it is exacted. There is some evidence that deterrence works – in other words that punishment is effective – on those who do not actually undergo it. The tutor is in one way in the same position as the doctor. Patients often feel they have not been treated unless they leave the surgery with a prescription. Teachers frequently feel that their referral has not been taken seriously unless the student receives some appropriate sanction. This matters because they will stop referring your students to you if they feel that 'nothing happens' when they do. What is more, students sometimes share that view, believing that if they are not punished they have 'got away with it'. There are two solutions: one is to punish offences and the other is to convince those around you that you are operating effectively even when you don't punish, or you can do both.

There are teachers who will never be convinced that behaviour can be altered without punishment. They will see only the failures and never notice the successes. Most teachers however tend to judge on results, and are fair-minded enough to recognise that no method of control or persuasion works every time. This takes time though, and as a new tutor it is probably better for your position with respect to both staff and students to punish offences thoughtfully, without a vestige of vengeance and with the consent if at all possible of the student. Once your position in the institution is established, no-one will care how you get your results as long as they are not noticeably worse than anyone else's. Those who have not offended will be deterred from doing so and the staff will continue to inform you of the misdeameanours of your tutees.

We need to explore the notion of punishment by consent. The teacher is in the position, if she wishes it, of an absolute dictator. She can impose rules arbitrarily and can invent and exact punishments at will to enforce obedience. If she does this, she is demonstrating the meaning of power and teaching the students an important lesson: if you are in a position where you can make other people do what you want them to do, then it is all right to ignore their wishes completely and make them obey you by whatever means. But you do not *have* to operate like this. You can, if you wish, be a benevolent dictator, so that while you retain absolute power, you rule in what you perceive to be the interests of the students. Or you can hand any degree of control to the students themselves.

This last position can be applied in any school context. It applies in a learning context, as we shall see in Chapter 3. We shall note its implications for recording in Chapter 6. In the context of punishment, it is initially based upon the recognition by the student that a fault has been committed, so that it may be worth using some time and energy in achieving that recognition, and indeed in creating a climate in which students feel able to admit to their faults. A large part of this climate depends upon the tutor's own capacity to recognise, admit to and apologise for his own mistakes. If the tutor is unable to shed the protective barrier which teachers have traditionally maintained and reveal himself as a flawed person, it is unlikely that anyone else in the group will be able to.

Once the student recognises that she was in the wrong in some respect, it becomes possible to negotiate an appropriate sanction. If possible it should genuinely fit the crime, and indeed provide recompense to the person, if there is one, who has been damaged by the offence. Students need to be able to empathise sufficiently with a teacher – for example, to see that public rudeness by a student damages her self-respect, and that a sincerely meant and well-made apology can give that self-respect back. The sanction applied should never take away the student's self-respect and nor should it leave her feeling resentful. If you sense that she feels the punishment is unjust or excessive, it may be worth exploring with her why she feels that.

In the end, of course, there will be times when you will need to apply sanctions which the student does not accept, but they should be rare and you should still be very clear that the sanction is just and not excessive.

SELF-EXPLORATION

Consider the following situations. What would you do? How would you feel?

1. Philip, a student in your tutor group (fourth year), is reported to you by the Deputy Head for failing to keep to school dress regulations. He persists, even after you have pointed it out to him.

2. Rebecca, a fifth-year student, fails to hand in homework after being consistently conscientious throughout the school. It happens again and again, always in the same subject.

3. Jayne is reported to you for smoking. On enquiry, she denies the offence, and she is a student whom you have previously learnt to trust.

4. A teacher asks you to deal with Tony who is misbehaving in his lessons. Tony is generally well behaved – if lively – with you, and you have a trusting relationship with him. You know that if you take it to your pastoral head, the student will be severely punished.

Chapter 3

Tutorial Groupwork

Introduction

The last few years have seen something of a revolution in many schools as the tutor has been asked to take on a structured teaching role with his tutor group. A number of strands lie behind this movement, many of which are by no means new. Before I go on to look at the practical implications for the tutor, it is worth asking what the philosophy behind the group tutorial is, so that in trying to implement it we do not take on more than will enhance the pastoral care that we provide.

First, there began to be a feeling in the 1970s that if pastoral care were to be done properly then there would be simply too much for the pastoral staff to cope with. Two solutions to this problem pointed to groupwork. One solution was to carry out some of the pastoral tasks with groups of students instead of with individuals. The other was to pass on the skills to solve problems to students so that they could deal with them themselves.

Second, there was the feeling that pastoral staff were spending all their time reacting to crises instead of looking at what was causing them and removing those factors. An approach which was preventive, or, to employ a later buzz-word, proactive, rather than reactive, seemed to be called for.

Third, and related to the first two points, was the sense that schools shouldn't offer to some students what they didn't offer to all. Pastoral care was being offered in general to a small number of students who had problems. What about all the students who did not have problems?

Fourth, several individuals and groups, notably Leslie Button, Douglas Hamblin, and Ken David and his Lancashire team including Jill Baldwin, had begun to work on an approach to classroom work which is now known as 'active learning'. Many of the methods were tried and tested and had been used by teachers of English and Humanities for a number of years, but the application of them to the tutor's work was innovatory.

Fifth, the active learning movement advocated a strong mutually supportive role to members of the tutor group, and provided practical approaches to helping groups of students to deal with their own problems, an objective which I mentioned above.

Finally, there was a growing sense among many teachers that the curriculum simply did not address the problems of everyday living, and that it could and should do so. From this concern developed a new curricular area called Personal and Social Education that would seek to fill the vacuum. The tutor involvement arises because it was felt by some that this highly sensitive and personal area of the curriculum, which would involve open expression of opinion by students and consequently require a more relaxed and accepting style from the teacher, would be best handled by a member of staff who had a special and personal relationship with the students.

What we have to do is to disentangle the various strands here and base our approach to group tutorial work on the precept that we should adopt and practise whatever contributes to the care which the tutor is able to provide for his individual students. Other aspects may be central educationally but do not necessarily form part of the responsibility of the teacher-tutor.

Having said this, we have to bear in mind that schools have not necessarily implemented tutorial groupwork in accordance with a similar philisophy, and the tutor may find himself being asked to teach as a tutor areas which in his view do not contribute to the quality of the care he can offer to his tutees. If he is told what to teach, he may well have to go ahead and teach it. However, I shall contribute more to method than to content in this chapter so he may find the methods suggested of use. I am in any case much more concerned with the tutor who is expected to do something but who is left in the dark as to what to do or how to do it.

While I understand the first three points, I am not wholly convinced by them. I endorse the feeling that pastoral care cannot be carried out effectively by year/house heads, but, as I have suggested elsewhere, the solution is to involve all staff as pastoral teachers. There are tasks which are quite inappropriate for groupwork and where individual counselling is essential. There are also such tasks as liaison with parents, other staff and other agencies, where time has to be found outside that put aside for the tutor to be with his tutor group.

Nor do I wholly sympathise with the view that it is possible to forestall most of the problems by allowing students to discuss or roleplay them in advance. The fact is that most of us only learn how to deal with a problem when we actually confront it, when it is, in other words, our problem; however carefully planned and executed the learning approach, it will mean that much less when the student hasn't personally experienced such a situation.

Again, to argue as the third point does that we should offer pastoral care to all students sounds like justice; we should not have a favoured few students who benefit from some aspect of the school's work in ways which others forgo. But we should be careful that we are not simply offering help to those who don't need it. Rejecting the reactive aspects of pastoral work on the grounds that not everyone benefits is like opposing Oxfam on the grounds that it does nothing to help the rich. We certainly need to ensure that all students who need whatever facility is available should have it, but we are not required to ensure that those who do not need it have it as well.

The growth of active learning has been of considerable benefit to schools and will continue to influence what goes on in the classroom. But we should not see it – nor do its proponents wish us to – as solely or even mainly applicable to the work of the tutor. Nor should the tutor feel that he cannot be eclectic: all learning methods have their value and we should not throw methods which do not come under the heading of active learning out of the window.

The final two points I endorse in general. The tutor group has an important role in supporting the student and providing a sympathetic social context for her development, and the tutor who can facilitate this kind of development is providing pastoral care of a high order. Much of the work which I advocate will have this as an aim.

The development of personal and social education (PSE) has done more to increase the relevance, both actual and perceived, of the curriculum than any other recent movement, and it is true that the tutor and his group have a role in approaching any area of learning which has a personal dimension. I am yet to be convinced that all PSE should come within a tutorial slot. Partly, it seems to me that a large proportion of what we call education ought to further the personal and social development of students, so to bracket off an area as 'PSE' may neither be helpful nor even accurate. Furthermore, the fact that a teacher knows a group of students well does not necessarily imply that he is the best person to teach some particular topic – or if it does then maybe we should ask why secondary schools aren't organised on the same lines as primary schools.

The term 'personal and social education' is sometimes used to imply active learning methods but there is no conceptual link, and indeed ruling out of PSE a method which is not active on those grounds would suggest that we couldn't show films, bring in outside lecturers or read from books. The personal dimensions of a topic, say, in health education are not the whole story. There are practical skills to be passed on and knowledge to be acquired. It may be that these will be taught using, among others, active learning methods, but I see no reason why they should not be taught by a PSE specialist in the same way as maths is taught by a maths specialist. However, there seems little doubt that discussion of the personal implications of what has been learnt is entirely appropriate for the tutor group, where close relatonships should be built up between tutor and student and between student and student.

The following practical section will, therefore, have two main aims: first, to introduce methods which contribute to the building of a friendly, sympathetic and supportive ethos for the tutor group; and second, to consider the personal dimension in issues in PSE.

Building a tutor group

The philosophical foundations of the groupwork movement are fairly homogeneous, even though a number of different people and institutions have played a part in its development. In general, though, the approach upon which this chapter is based is that followed by the Counselling and Career Development Unit of the University of Leeds, and which may be found set out in greater detail in *Lifeskills Teaching* (Hopson and Scally, 1981).

What is distinctive about the tutor group is, first, that the sense which its members have of its own identity, unity and mutual supportiveness is a large part of the purpose of the groupwork, rather than just a means to an end; and second, that the group's existence is long term, ideally even for the five years during which its members are at the school. The building of the group is therefore of signal importance.

The first thing to recognise is that your tutor group is composed of a number of individuals who are all very different, who come together only at certain times, who have very different experiences in between those meetings, and who might not under natural circumstances wish to be together at all. Teachers tend to talk facilely of a 'good group' or a 'bad group', or even to place on a group a more discrete personality – a group with a good sense of humour or a sulky group. These qualities are not illusory, but they are equally not applicable to every member of the group: they arise from the personalities of some of the more dominant members. Thus, to speak as if they were is at best to ignore those members who do not share the 'group quality' and at worst liable to lead to injustice. Keeping a class in for being noisy is a crude example of this: there are always students who were not noisy. We should never lose an awareness of the individuals who make up the group. The group in itself has no intrinsic worth: it is of value only as long as it services its members.

Second, building a group is an ongoing process. You don't build it and then leave it alone. There will always be occasions when you will feel the need to re-emphasise the identity and mutuality of the group, particularly at such times as returning to school after holidays, but also when there are circumstances laying stress on group relationships.

The third point is that the activities which we do with a group should always have a clear purpose – other than filling a slot in the timetable. This is a problem to the tutor who has had no say in the allocation of a period of time to a tutorial period, but it is in the tutor's interests as much as the students' that the activities are purposive: foisting activities which demand a level of commitment and involvement on students when such activities don't have a clear rationale is a rapid route to student apathy and lack of co-operation. In the exercises outlined below the purpose is stated first, and it should also be stated first to the students.

Methods and materials

GROUP-BUILDING EXERCISES

1. Self-disclosure
Purpose: To introduce the new group to each other and to encourage interest in others.

Basic exercise: The students each write six things that they would like the group to know about them on postcards. The cards are mixed up and dealt to the group. Each student reads out the card she has in turn and the group guesses to whom it applies. Once correctly identified, the group can question the student who wrote the card for further details.

Modifications: The cards can be ranged on the floor or a table, and students select one which interests them to read out. They can later partner the person selected.

2. Twos and fours
Purpose: To help each student to make contact with three others and to encourage listening to each other.

Basic exercise: Students are in pairs and each partner is given two minutes to talk about herself. The pair joins up with another pair and each student introduces her partner. Her partner must not interrupt or correct her during the introduction, though of course she can when she has finished.

Variations: Where the exercise is aimed towards rebuilding relationships, the topic can be changed: what I did over the holidays, how I planned my revision, etc.

3. Autobiography
Purpose: To find out about each other's life outside school.

Basic exercise: Produce a large, fairly detailed map of the area (street names aren't necessary); the Ordnance Survey 1:25000 is suitable, enlarged if possible. Students find places of importance to them on it:

1. Where I live.
2. Where I was born (though bear in mind that quite a number of students will have been born outside the area so they will need space on the border of the map to write this in).
3. A place where I would like to be now.
4. A place that means a lot to me.

Each student talks about her places (those she wishes to talk about).

Variations: A map of Britain can be used to talk about holidays. Be careful not to expose students for whom locating places is difficult and stressful. If the tutor goes first, he can be careful himself not to find his own places too easily (for some tutors, modelling geographical incompetence will present no problems!)

4. Shifting sub-groups
Purpose: Membership of different groups, expressing preferences, accepting differences.

Basic exercise: This exercise is about differences between people but differences which are selected – that is, preferences. For example, people who like garlic at one end of the room, people who don't at the other; colour preferences (red, blue, yellow, green); tea/coffee; county preferences (use names of four counties in another part of the country, selecting those which have no strong image (eg avoid Cornwall, Cumbria, Merseyside); paper/stone/metal/wood, etc. Discuss those which get chosen most and least, being careful to value those with unusual preferences.

Variations: If you want to end up with groups of equal sizes, it is best to phrase the preferences so that there are differences of degree, such as: 'If you absolutely detest Scotland, sit at this end of the circle and if you absolutely love it sit at that end; the rest, spread yourselves in between according to how you feel about it.' You can then put people next to each other in, for example, fours or pairs. Keep the preferences innocuous, unless there is some reason for wanting them to sit in a particular way – for instance, you might want people of similar views to sit together, or separately. A horseshoe may be the best formation for this exercise. This is described in more detail in the section on grouping arrangements.

5. Greeting

Purpose: Self-knowledge and awareness of others.

Basic exercise: Students walk round the room. They should greet as many people as possible and say something about themselves to each other in a sentence.

Variations: The first time round the room, students can be told that they mustn't look at each other.

TEACHING METHODS FOR GROUPWORK

1. Lecturettes

Hardly a new method, but one which decidedly has its place. It is, in fact, essential to start by explaining the purpose of the activity, which means a sort of lecturette at the beginning. Always remember that most people have an average attention span of about 10 minutes, so it is important to avoid exceeding that limit.

Rather than producing a fully fledged lecturette, it can be an effective teaching technique to make a single point clearly and pithily, and then to ask the group to break up into sub-groups and discuss it. Then the next point is made and so on.

While giving any lecture, it is a good idea to stop after each main point made to allow the students an opportunity to turn to the person next to them and discuss it. This can give them the opportunity to judge whether they have missed or not understood anything.

2. Structured discussion

This is a well-established approach too, but it is important to make sure the structure is tight so that it is purposive. It is generally best to intervene at each stage to keep the discussion to schedule. Students are split into sub-groups which can consist of between three and ten members.

A suitable schedule is as follows:

1. Teacher sets aims clearly to group.
2. Teacher writes up stimulus questions on board or flipchart.
3. Students make notes individually (two mins).
4. Each person in sub-group states views for two minutes without interruption.
5. Open discussion in sub-group.
6. Sub-group decides what to report back.
7. Plenary: sub-groups report back.

3. Brainstorming

This is a popular and very effective technique for making lists quickly so that a group isn't held up by not being able to think of anything 'really good' to write. It is also particularly good in encouraging everyone in the group to feel that their idea will be accepted.

A 'scribe' is appointed who will write everything down. The key word is 'everything', since *all* ideas are written down on the sheet of paper, no matter how silly. No discussion or evaluation or selection is allowed during the brainstorm.

The brainstorm can, of course, be followed up by discussion of the points listed.

4. Roleplay

The main function of roleplay is to practise stressful or sensitive situations in a safe context. Most people are wary of engaging in it, believing either, wrongly, that it required innate talents or, rightly, that it can be dangerous. The roleplay therefore needs to be approached cautiously and, most importantly, there needs to be plenty of time for discussion of how students felt about it – debriefing – when it is complete.

Example: A student in each pair is asked to select a misdemeanour that she has committed in school recently, and to imagine that she has to explain her behaviour to a teacher. Her partner roleplays the teacher. Students then exchange roles. In this way, they can then discuss their feelings in each situation, and talk about how they might have explained themselves better.

Variations: Roleplay is a useful technique, and because it is also a powerful one it needs to be carefully employed. The distinction between roleplay and simulation is generally held to be that in a roleplay you play someone else whereas in a simulation you operate as yourself but in a fictitious situation. Thus, a well-known simulation is one where participants have to choose a use for a bomb site, each participant functioning as a member of a special interest group – the local tradespeople or a playgroup, for instance. The personality of a participant is not specified so it will be her own.

In a roleplay, the personality may be important to the context. For instance, someone might have to play a student who is in trouble for disrupting a lesson, which might presuppose personality characteristics. The above example required one student of the pair to be a teacher. It is important, though, to stress that students need to have a real teacher in mind (though they don't have to say who it is!). This should avoid the possibility of caricature which leads to stereotyped responses. Stereotyping prevents real learning in roleplay.

It should be recognised that there are dangers in roleplay, in that it is possible to confront real emotions that a person has been able to avoid. There may also be confusion between the role and the real person, so that anger or other emotions aroused during the roleplay need to be fully talked through, either in the group as a whole, between the people engaged in the roleplay, or privately between student and tutor.

5. Case study
This is an approach to problem solving involving the use of a specific case to illustrate a problematic situation and stimulate discussion of it, and can be used to complement or as an alternative to roleplay. The fact that it is specific means that, just as with a play or novel, it is possible to identify with the protagonists.

6. Critical incident
This activity is similar to a case study, but because it presents less detail regarding time, place and character, it allows the student to imagine herself in the situation. A general description of a type of situation is given and the students discuss how they would behave or react.

Example: You are unjustly accused of stealing £5 from the teacher's desk. How would you respond to the teacher's accusation? What results might your response have?

7. Exercises/games

Some of the group-building work would come into the category of games and exercises. The important thing is that, to provide useful learning, most games need to be followed by reflection and discussion.

8. Tapes

Sometimes it can be a useful stimulus to have a tape of a discussion or roleplay made in advance. This enables the teacher to focus on group organisation rather than on, say, reading a passage aloud; it also means that you can get the stimulus just right, because you can re-record if you are not satisfied with the result.

9. Worksheets/questionnaires

Douglas Hamblin (in conversation) warns against the 'death of a thousand worksheets', and he is absolutely right. They have sometimes been seen as a panacea, probably because they can be presented to a group without introduction and the group can then be left to fill them in individually. This allows the teacher to insist on silence, which is often easier and less threatening than encouraging talk. Educationally, such sessions are in themselves of little value, and students very rapidly become bored and disaffected. Even so, a questionnaire of the most elementary kind can introduce a topic for discussion. When the students have filled it in, they can come together in pairs or fours and discuss their answers.

Another approach is the 'open-ended aural questionnaire' (John Pearce's (1986) term). Here, questions are asked orally and a lot of time is given for the students to write their answers on their own. Where the topic is sensitive, this can be a way of encouraging students to think through their ideas without fear of having to disclose them to the group. It is essential to reassure students about the intended readership beforehand (usually the teacher). There needs to be a readership of some kind, otherwise the exercise feels rather sterile to the writer.

EXAMPLE

Where are you now?
An open-ended aural questionnaire
suitable for the opening session of
a course on personal relationships

Students are given two sheets of A4 lined paper. Then the whole of the following is spoken out loud to the class:

'I am going to give you the opportunity to write about some quite personal subjects. You may very well not have written anything like this before. As the questions are quite personal, you will need some assurances from me about what use is to be made of what you write.

'The first thing to say is that I shall not show what you have written to anyone else – not to teachers or pupils or parents, not even to my own family. When I have read what you have written, I shall make a comment if I feel there is one to be made, or I might answer any questions or problems which you have raised. But I shall not speak to you about what you have written or mention it again unless you ask me to. I shall simply give the sheets back to you next week, and they will be your property to do with what you like – throw them away if you wish, or discuss them with your parents, perhaps, or a very close friend.

'Each section of the questionnaire begins with a main question. As soon as you understand the main question, you may start writing; from time to time I shall ask other questions which may give you further ideas about what to write.

'Please do not consult anyone else about what you write. What goes down on to paper should be purely your own ideas. Try to be absolutely honest about what you write. As the lesson goes on, you may feel that you don't want anyone else to see what you have written; this will show that you are really trying to explore yourself.

'You may have virtually as much time as you like. If you want to carry on writing about a particular section while I am moving on to the next one, you may do so.'

The questions are then asked out loud, leaving ample pauses (anything from 3 to 15 minutes) in between each question. Subsidiary questions are thrown in while the students are writing.

A. You

How do you see yourself? what sort of person are you?

Describe your personality. Perhaps you could list your good and bad points. Do you like yourself? Is there anything you would like to be different about yourself? What sort of person would you like to be? You can name a person who is that sort of person if you wish. What qualities does s/he have which you admire?

B. School

How well do you cope with school?

I don't mean just the lessons, though you should mention how you get on with the work. But also think about how well you cope with mixing with a lot of other people, some of whom you may not like. And how well do you get on with the teachers? What about the routine of school life, with everything being timetabled?

C. Parents/guardians

How well do you get on with you parents or guardians?

Do you have enough freedom? Enough privacy? Do your ideas and opinions differ widely from those of your parents? (On clothes, music, political or religious issues, what is acceptable behaviour, etc). What about relationships with other members of the family?

D. Friends and boy/girlfriends

Are you happy with the friendships you have?

Which are more important to you – friends or girl/boyfriends? Do you have any difficulties with either kind of friendship?

E. The future

What do you want to achieve in your life?

Think of personal, social and career achievements. How far will you be able to control whether you can achieve them? What kinds of things do you worry about?

F. Understanding sex

How knowledgeable do you think you are about sex?

Where have you mainly learnt about sex? Are there any questions or problems which you would like answered during this course? What do you hope this course will do for you?

G. Evaluation

Now look back over what you have written. Is there anything you would like to add to any section? Have a look particularly at the first question, which you started when you were 'cold'. Now write a short paragraph about how you have felt about answering this questionnaire.

Steve Adams
Anne Hall

(Revised 31/1/87)

GROUPING ARRANGEMENTS

The shape of the room and the way the group is organised is very important in that it very often determines the kind of work which can be done. Students ranged in the traditional classroom pattern of serried ranks are separated from the teacher and focused on her. They therefore expect whatever happens to emanate from her and to be told exactly what they have to do and when. In such a setting the authority of the teacher is expected to be total, and if it is not for any reason the group will be unclear about the rules; it is often in such an ambiguous situation that behaviour problems occur (this point is graphically made in Hargreaves (1967)).

It is therefore worth putting a fair amount of thought into how you arrange your tutor base, and it is best if you are able and willing to regard the furniture as there to be moved. Tables are rarely helpful since they form barriers between participants and also encourage students to sprawl, which rarely helps to make a session purposive.

An example of how to form groups using student preferences can be found in the section on Group-Building on p 61. Groups don't have to be based on preferences, of course, though if they are to be based on individual characteristics you need to be certain that you don't touch any sensitive areas – at least unless you are ready and able to pick them up. For instance, grouping according to size may be stressful for a small student while grouping according to number of family members may be difficult for those whose family situation is unorthodox or where there has been a recent upheaval.

I often group students in a horseshoe formation – see p 68 for some examples of criteria that can be used for positioning students. Such methods of arranging the class, though simple, actually give the group members an opportunity to talk to a number of people in order to sort themselves out, and that it is a way of breaking the ice. It is also a way of raising energy, which is important at the beginning of the day or after a break when people (not just students!) tend to be lethargic.

There are times when self-selected groups are most appropriate, particularly when the topic of conversation is sensitive or when the mode of exercise itself is stressful – a roleplay, for instance. Self-selected pairs are frequently effective. With larger groups it is important to ensure that no-one gets left out – the strongest argument against self-selection.

Whenever the furniture is moved around it is of course important to be aware of the effect that you may have on colleagues. Students should be discouraged from dragging furniture, since apart from any damage to flooring it can disturb other classes. Most important, unless you are in your own teaching room, furniture should always be moved back to the arrangement in which you found it.

1. Circle

This speaks for itself. As with King Arthur's Round Table, it implies equality of all members. It is a good way to begin, therefore, and also to end. There is no reason why the tutor, sitting in the circle, shouldn't introduce a topic from that position.

2. Horseshoe

Equality is implied for the members of the group but it allows them to focus upon the teacher (though of course the 'teacher' need not be the teacher). This is a particularly appropriate formation when displaying discussion points on the blackboard or overhead projector.

The horseshoe, as already mentioned, is also a useful formation for initial grouping. If you regard the ends of the horseshoe as the extremes of a continuum with all the gradations in between, then you can ask students to order themselves around the horseshoe according to an almost infinite variety of criteria.

Try dates of birth – one end of the horseshoe is the nearest date of birth to 1 January in the class and the other end is the nearest to 31 December. Another simple one is door numbers, the lowest at one end and the highest at the other. If some students' homes have only names take them after the numbers in alphabetical order.

Criteria which concern preferences make good energy raisers, as well as being appropriate for random grouping. Ask students to think of their favourite place in the world – somewhere they have been or not, as they wish. Then ask them to sit so that the person whose favourite place is nearest the room you are working in is at one end of the horseshoe and the person whose favourite place is furthest from the room is at the other. You can then go round the horseshoe asking the students where they are in the world.

You can use physical features to order students, but they should be innocuous ones – best to avoid height, for instance. Hair colour is generally a good one, as long as there is a good variety of shades, and as long as there are no students who are self-conscious about the colour of their hair – some redheaded students may be. It is best to let the group order themselves: there is no need for you to be involved. They can negotiate in difficult cases: ask several people to give an opinion about which of two brown-haired students is the darker.

Once the horseshoe is ordered, you can group students by asking them to work with the student/s next to whom they are sitting.

3. Carousel

This is a useful technique for allowing students to listen to a range of different views on a particular topic. On dealing with bullying, for instance, students could receive possible strategies from several people and offer their own solutions to the reactions of several others. I recommend strongly that the stages mentioned below for building the double circle are followed, since they avoid confusion in what is quite a complex piece of classroom organisation.

Basic exercise: The students begin seated in a complete circle facing inwards. Students are given letters A and B alternately. It is a good idea to get them to shout out their letter so as to be sure that they know which they are. Then ask the Bs to move their chairs into the circle and sit so that they are each facing an A, thereby forming an outward looking smaller circle inside the first circle.

Students are now given a topic to discuss. It could be 'Where and when I do my homework'. Pairs seated opposite each other exchange ideas on the topic for two minutes. Then each student moves one place to her left, so that she is now seated opposite someone new and is two places from the person she was talking to last. Students now share ideas on the same topic with their new partners. This can be repeated several times – though not too often or students will become bored with saying the same thing, even though they are listening to different things. A plenary in which good ideas which students have learnt are shared is appropriate to end with.

Variations: A valuable use of this technique is for simple roleplay of stressful situations. For instance, you are late home from a party and your parents are waiting up when you arrive. What will you say? The partner plays the parent. This way the student can modify her behaviour on a new partner after testing it out unsuccessfully on the previous one. However, it is important that everyone gets a crack at both roles, so after at most three partner changes the roles themselves should be changed. I find it best to ask students to change from inside to outside circle, and vice versa, to represent the change of role – though if you do this you should remember that students now need to move one seat to their *right* rather than left or they will be back with a previous partner.

4. Twos/fours

This is simply an approach to discussion which enables every student to contribute. It can be carried further in that fours can combine into eights, and the eights report back the group's thinking to plenary. The example below uses twos and fours in a slightly different way, to allow some degree of disclosure in a safe context, which will ultimately lead to tolerance and a valuing of individual differences among the members of the group.

EXAMPLE

Purpose

To learn about and accept differences between members of the group.

Basic exercise

1. In pairs: What differences are there between you and your partner? How do you look different? What differences are there in what you like doing? What differences are there in what you are good at?

2. Join into fours. Tutor to hand out slips of paper, approx. 2in × 6in. Each member of the group then individually writes four statements on four slips of paper which s/he thinks are true of her/him alone of the group members (a maximum of one statement should concern appearance).

3. The slips are laid face down in the middle of the group in four piles. In turn, each member of the group takes one of her/his slips. Group negotiates as to whether s/he is to be allowed to keep it (only if it is true of her/him and only of her/him out of the members of the group can s/he keep it).

4. Divide a flipchart into four segments. Write the names of the four members in the four segments. Then stick the agreed statements in the correct segment, and display chart.

Variations

If the whole group know each other, a plenary negotiation can take place. Group can walk around and look at the slips that the fours have given themselves, and then any comments can be made to the whole group. Other differences might also be raised. It is important that all this is done in a spirit of valuing differences, not picking out peculiarities. If there is any likelihood of the latter attitude, the plenary should be avoided. The group attitude should be: Aren't we lucky to have such a variety of people in our group!

It is a good idea to start off with a group-building exercise (such as the one cited earlier on shifting sub-groups) which also concerns valuing differences.

5. Trios

Arranging the group in threes can be simply an alternative to pairs or fours. Threes can then combine into sixes. But there are certain activities where threes are particularly appropriate.

One of these is where you want a discussion taking place between a pair to be observed and the pair to be given feedback on what went on in the discussion. The observer can be given notes to work from which ask her to attend to particular aspects of the discussion. For instance: Who did the most talking? Who asked the most questions? How much disagreement was there? How did each person behave when they disagreed?

A second use of threes is where the group would benefit from very attentive listening. Each member of the three is allowed to talk for a set time on whatever the topic is, while the other two listen closely. They can then question the speaker to clarify her thinking.

6. Fishbowl

This requires the group to divide into two sub-groups. One sub-group sits in the centre of the room to discuss a topic while the outer sub-group observes them. They may take notes according to some guidelines laid down by the teacher, as suggested for trios. At the end of the discussion the outer circle give the inner circle feedback about the way they worked, what roles people adopted, how successful they were, and so on.

Another use of this formation is where the inner sub-group is asked to complete a task – building a stand out of paper to support a tumbler, for example – and the outer sub-group is asked to observe the way the inner sub-group organises itself to complete the task. Questions which the outer sub-group might be asked to answer could include: Which members of the group made suggestions? Did anyone lead the group? What ideas were rejected? How quckly did the group find a solution? Did all members of the group contribute and how?

It may be a good idea to give the members of the observing group specific tasks – two people observing the process of the task and two observing the roles the members of the task group play. The notes shown in Figures 1 and 2 can be given to the observing group.

7. Shifting sub-groups

The basic purpose of 'shifting sub-groups' is as a method of sharing thinking between groups (see the section on sharing ideas on pp 74–5). Where a group has been discussing a particular topic in fours, a pair from each four can combine with a pair from another four to create a new four,

---

FISHBOWL

Notes for observers 1

Map the progress of the task.
   Note early stages, movement, key ideas,
   changes of direction, hold-ups, irrelevant
   diversions, acceleration, key stages in
   solving task, etc.

Figure 1. *Fishbowl – notes for observers 1*

FISHBOWL

Notes for observers 2

Note roles played by group members.
   Look for ideas person, instruction follows,
   leader, joker, silent person, diverter, talker,
   expert, person who keeps group on task, etc.
   (Find some of your own.)
   Remember that one person may function
   within several roles at different stages
   of the task.

Figure 2. *Fishbowl – notes for observers 2*

giving the new sub-group the opportunity to experience a new point of view.

8. Panels

This is a form of structure for discussion in which questions on a particular topic are addressed to a panel, who can comprise teachers, students from another tutor group, members of the group, or a mixture.

If the panel consists of members of the group, it can be changed if a member of the 'audience' wishes to replace a panel-member. She could either raise her hand, or touch the panel-member whom she wishes to replace.

9. Teaching/learning groups

This is a useful learning method, but is also a way of removing the feeling that only the teacher teaches or that the teacher has all the answers.

One group which has acquired some information or skill combines with another which hasn't and takes on the task of passing it on. It can be done by one member of the teaching group leading and the others chipping in, or by the 'teachers' being paired with the learners. If the learning groups include teaching staff, the distinction between teachers and students can be effectively reduced.

10. Individual work

Certain tasks are best done individually, while many others benefit by some individual thinking and/or note-making being done initially before group discussion commences. We have seen how this applies with questionnaires in the section on teaching methods.

EXAMPLE

Purpose

To plan a revision schedule.

Basic exercise

Planning tasks are particularly amenable to individual work. Students need to be given a blank calendar covering the remaining weeks up to the exams. Whether you divide the weeks into days depends upon how close the exams are. A blank sheet of paper, even ruled with a grid, is less effective as it tends to make the task seem less manageable.

Individually, students begin to fill in (preferably in pencil so that it can be rubbed out and thus writing something down is less final and therefore easier) which topics – not just subjects – they might revise in which weeks or days. When they have finished this draft, they can join up with partner to discuss their plans. After discussion, they return to their own plan, modify it, and then commit themselves to it by filling it in in ink.

Variations

The same sort of approach can be used for making a schedule for any task. Younger students finding it difficult to organise homework into their after-school activities might use it to plan their evening.

A simple instrument for a student (or anyone, in fact) setting targets for a difficult task is to set out what she intends to do:

- this week;
- before the end of term;
- by the end of the year;

or whatever time limit is appropriate – in other words, a short-, a medium- and a long-term goal.

SHARING IDEAS
Sometimes simply going through the process of thinking or talking some topic through is sufficient, but often it is valuable both in itself and as an incentive to give opportunities for groups to share their thinking with one another. The following are some ways of doing this.

1. Display
Groups pin up their flipcharts and all the students walk round and look at what other groups have produced. This is a simple solution to the problem of how to share. It has perhaps the disadvantage that the business of looking at another group's flipchart may not be unduly interesting in itself.

2. Passing round
Groups pass on their flipcharts to the next group. This is similar to the display method but it has the advantage that it keeps the group together so that they can discuss what they are looking at and decide whether to use ideas from another group as they are looking. It is slightly more time-consuming because the sheets then have to be passed on to the next group.

3. *Adding on*

Each group has a flipchart which deals with a different issue. When they have written down their thoughts, they pass on the sheet for the next group to read and add to, and they receive a different issue from another group. Students need to be reminded to write their own comments, not to alter comments made by other groups. As this activity progresses the length of time for reading will be greater, but for writing less, because more points will have been made.

This is a good method in that it provides a motive for reading as students are looking to see what they can add. On the other hand, it requires the same number of topics as groups, which may have to be contrived.

4. *Joining up groups*

The simplest and often most effective sharing comes from combining groups. Pairs can join into fours, fours into eights and so on. The thinking from two groups can thus be shared by the new larger group. The logical extent of this method is the following:

5. *Reporting back to plenary*

This can either be done by one member from each sub-group reporting back the group's ideas, or by each individual student making a brief comment, perhaps in a sentence. Students who feel they have nothing to add may 'pass'.

Big groups are threatening to some people, thus the plenary may be an opportunity for only those who enjoy an audience to participate. For this reason it should not be employed exclusively.

6. *Shifting sub-groups*

As I mentioned above, at the end of a period in which the group has been discussing in sub-groups of, say, four, each pair from each four can join up with a pair from another four. They can then share ideas with the new four. If they started in pairs, before joining into fours, the new pairs can be different from those which began:

1. Pairs: AB   CD   EF   GH
2. Fours: ABCD   EFGH
3. New fours: ACEG   BDFH

7. *Delegates*

This is where one member of each sub-group goes to tell another group what they have decided on some issue. This is a good first step if the group as a whole are aiming to negotiate a decision – for example, which of a range of activities they are going to do. It is limited in that it takes some time for each sub-group to have heard the delegate from every other sub-group, so it works best when the tutor group is divided into, say, three large groups. Another problem is that it depends on the capacity of the delegate to report coherently on the decision of her sub-group – though this may provide some useful learning about selection!

CONTRACTING AND EVALUATION

It may seem surprising to some teachers that there might be any mileage in agreeing with students what a session might comprise. Traditionally, one might suppose, teachers are there to force students to do what they are there to avoid. On the other hand, from two standpoints it makes sense to do so.

First, don't students like anyone else have the right to a say in what experiences they are to be put through? And second, if we are actually expecting them to make an active contribution to the lesson, aren't we expecting a lot from them if they haven't been given an opportunity even to express a view on the topic or approach?

To refer to what goes on at the beginning of a set of lessons as a contract might seem legalistic and indeed an overstatement of the actual procedure, but what the term does do is to expose the fact that students in any context either consent to take part in classroom activities or not. Using the term impels us to make explicit what we are intending to do so that students' willingness to co-operate can likewise be made clear.

The contract has basically two parts to it: first, there is the explanation by the tutor of what he intends to do, what the purpose of the activity is, and how he intends to do it; and secondly, there is the opportunity for the students to ask questions, state their objectives and make suggestions or alterations to either content, order or methods.

A first principle is that the contract has got to be genuine, so if the tutor has boundaries which are not open to discussion – not negotiable – there should be no pretence that they are. At the most obvious level, the tutor will not be prepared to negotiate whether the students are present or not. More contentiously, he needs to decide whether and under what circumstances individual students can opt out of an activity.

Contracting is not something a teacher either does or not. There are degrees. With a group of adults, say, or sixth-formers, who may have their own very clear objectives (agenda, as in counselling, is an apt term here) for the session, it is beneficial to give them the opportunity to discuss and make explicit, preferably in writing, what they are. Younger students, particularly in schools where giving responsibility to students for their own learning is unfamiliar, will need to be introduced gradually to the idea that they can have some control over what happens.

Simple written statements of objectives, at best a sub-group statement produced after discussion, are effective in focusing the students' subsequent activity. A question asking what the student hopes to learn from a lesson or series of lessons is a minimal contract. Such a question can only be answered once the tutor has explained clearly what is to take place, and what his objectives for the session are.

Within a framework in which students work in groups, making explicit what the student hopes or expects gives her the opportunity to make a contribution to ensuring that it happens – or if it does not to accept some responsibility for its not happening.

The following questions comprise an 'expectations sheet'.

1. What do you hope to get out of this lesson/course/module?

2. What worries or concerns do you have about this lesson/course/module?

3. What do you need from the teacher and from your fellow students?

4. What do you intend to do in this lesson/course/module to help you to achieve your objective?

The second question is important in bringing to the surface any fears which the students may have, and the third and fourth questions remind the students that it is not only the teacher but also themselves who have responsibility for the learning which may take place.

If you want to be able to respond to the students' objectives by modifying the course to suit them, you will need to give them the opportunity to feed their ideas to you, preferably on to a big sheet of paper rather than the board so that you can keep it. Alternatively, you can put them into four groups and give each group one question from the expectations sheet to answer. Using the sharing approach called 'adding on' each group can contribute to each of the four sheets, which can then be displayed on the wall.

Even if you decide not to change the lesson in the light of students' comments, it is still useful for them to express their expectations, both to bring them to the surface and as a focus for the evaluation which they can produce at the end of the lesson. Here again, some teachers may be unsure about the notion that students should evaluate the lesson. Once more, part of the answer is to say that students surely have a right to express a view on what they have experienced; they will anyway and it is likely to be of more value if it is passed on to the teacher.

Second, part of the objection which teachers may have is based upon the idea that the evaluation is all about the student assessing the competence of the teacher. This presupposes a view of the teacher as the purveyor of knowledge from whom all answers flow, whereas, at least in the context of the kind of work we are discussing, this is not an accurate image. The tutor may set the topic and framework for the activity – so he certainly carries some responsibility but the students have far more responsibility than under a more didactic regime for what they learn, not only because they have been given an opportunity to give their views and influence the shape of the session but also because they are active participants in the whole process.

Thirdly, a large part of the evaluation is not to assess the session as good or bad, but for the student to reflect upon what she has learnt. To make explicit what is often not clarified is a benefit to learning in itself. If, for example, during evaluation the student is able to state that she learnt from a friend how she deflects unpleasant teasing, she is more likely to benefit from that insight if she articulates it than if she is not given the opportunity to recognise that she has learnt it.

As with contracting, there are degrees. At its most systematic, students can answer a detailed questionnaire containing questions on content, method, factors contributing to and inhibiting learning, and so on. A simple form of evaluation, however, might be something along the lines of the following:

- *What have you found useful/interesting in this session?*

- *What would you like to cover further?*

- *Any other comments?*

Note that the focus is on the learning not the teaching, though the tutor has to be prepared to receive comments about his contribution, and he is expecting too much if he wants them all to be favourable.

Sometimes, simply allowing everyone to make a comment at the end, orally in plenary, is sufficient, especially if the topic is incomplete and is to be continued.

If you have used the expectations sheet given above, all that it is necessary to ask is:

How far have your expectations been realised?

and add:

Any other comments you wish to make?

Another approach is to give all students a diary so that they can make their own regular notes about what they have learnt. It can be addressed to the tutor if he wishes – or if the student wishes – and read frequently by him if the student and tutor agree that it should be. However, opportunity must be given for diary-writing during the session if it is to be done. It is unrealistic to expect this to happen unless time is put aside for it; it won't take long for the student to realise where the tutor places the diary in his priorities if he does not allow time for it within the session.

CONTENT

As I said in the introduction, it may very well be that the topics which the tutor is to cover with his group will be laid down by the head of year/house or by the senior management.If so, then on the one hand it is one less problem for the tutor to solve, though on the other it means that he has less control over what goes on in the tutorial – and may have to explain this as one of the non-negotiable areas when contracting. I offer the following for tutors operating in schools where there is no such guidance.

It is useful to think in terms of what may be covered as coming under the following categories, irrespective of what age the students are.

1. Personal awareness
Purpose: To develop an understanding and acceptance of myself as an individual, including a recognition of my capacities and the important needs and wants which motivate me and influence my decision-making.

Suggested topics:

Handling stress	Safety
Health and hygiene	Independence
Self-assessment	Leisure
Self-confidence	Personal organisation
Decision-making	Goal-setting
Drug use	Handling change
Achievements	Coping with emotions
Physical development	Being straight
Self-discipline	

2. Personal relationships

Purpose: To develop an understanding of the range of human relationships, with a stress on close friendships and romantic/sexual relationships.

Suggested topics:

Sensitivity to others	Peer group pressure
Responsibility	Sexual relationships
Tolerance	Media pressure
Discrimination	Community awareness
Honesty	Respect
Moral issues	Family relationships
Gender equity	Friendship
Rules	Loyalty
Meeting people	Working as a team
Problem page	Leadership
Relationships within the group	Co-operating
Listening	Group decision making
The environment	

3. Social skills and awareness

Purpose: To develop an understanding and recognition of the needs and wants of others, and to consider ways of behaving which take them into account while allowing me to retain power over my own situation.

Suggested topics:

Communication	Asking for help
Humour	Handling teachers
Assertiveness	Handling reprimands
Accepting criticism	Handling aggressive people
Giving constructive feedback	Handling authority

4. Study skills and curriculum support

Purpose: To support the work of subject departments by developing strategies which improve efficiency in study, applicable across the curriculum.

Suggested topics:

Note-taking	Motivation
Homework	Exam technique
Time-management	Revision
Planning and organisation	Essay planning
Setting out work	Style
Where I can get help	Oral skills

5. Careers
Purpose: To relate personal needs, wants and capacities to what is available for me to do after leaving school.

Suggested topics:

Options planning	Decision making
Self-assessment	Assessing pressures
Work experience monitoring	How to get information

6. The school
Purpose: To ensure that all students get the most out of the institution.

Suggested topics:

Induction	Mapping the school
Functions of staff	Using my parents
Understanding the curriculum	School rules
Clubs and societies	Where can I get ...?

Some of the above topics are clearly to be located at a particular stage of development or of schooling. An example of the former is puberty and of the latter, options planning. Most, however, are recurring. That is to say, they are not simply covered at one stage and then finished, but are built on year by year – the so-called 'spiral curriculum'.

VERTICAL TUTOR GROUPS
A vertical system is one where the pastoral unit contains students of different age groups. The most common of these systems is the house system. It is possible to have a house system within which the tutor groups are horizontal – that is, they contain students from one year group only – but many house systems operate with all-age tutor groups as well, so that there are, say, half a dozen students from each year in each group.

If only because I have worked with all-age groups myself, it is important that some mention be made of them. It is probably because they make groupwork more difficult that house systems have become less fashionable but there are many advantages in the vertical system – in breaking down barriers, encouraging a less hierarchical approach, militating against bullying, facilitating help from older for younger students, and so on.

There are two ways of coping with groupwork in a vertical group: one is to exploit the fact that you have a range of ages and therefore of interests, experience and viewpoints; the other is to break down the group into its component parts and deal with the four to six students in a particular year on their own.

If the tutor always practises the latter approach, two difficulties follow. First, what is to be done with the students to whom he is not attending? And secondly, how is he going to find the time to cover all the students in his group? Both problems may be solved for you centrally. The head of house may be able and willing to take charge of some of the years with whom you are not working – for instance, by taking an assembly with two or three house/year groups. She may also provide a schedule so that you know on which day you are to work with which group, and the school may provide sufficient time within the week for you to work with all age-groups.

The approach of working with all ages together avoids these difficulties, but there are some topics – such as personal relationships or options choices, for instance – which are unsuitable for being covered by all the years together. Even so, most topics and approaches are suitable for groups of two or three different years. Fourth- and fifth-year students, for example, can be invaluable in giving information and advice to third-year students choosing their options. Second-year students can work with the new entry to help them to cope with the early weeks at the school. Problems of puberty can be covered within an all-age context, though for some topics the tutor might wish to take the sexes separately to encourage a greater frankness (this is not always necessary, however, as there are advantages in the boys being aware of the girls' problems, and vice versa).

Most of the approaches and exercises explained in the first five sections of this chapter are as applicable to the vertical as to the horizontal tutor group, especially when it is remembered that most horizontal groups are mixed ability and therefore the range of interests and competences might be felt to be hardly any less wide. The possibilities for mutual assistance in a vertical group are greater, however, so if it is possible to overcome the problems associated with the content, with flexibility and planning, the benefits might outweigh the difficulties even in groupwork.

Chapter 4

Getting Help

In the day-to-day situations which the tutor will meet from the start in dealing with his tutees, he generally has the option of taking action himself or getting help from someone else. Often it requires as much skill to bring someone else in as it does to deal with the situation oneself. I shall discuss some of the skills which are required for helping students individually in the next chapter. In this chapter, we shall be concerned with the skills of referral.

Referral: when, to whom, how

'To refer' means to consult someone else about a problem, situation or case. It tends to get used to mean to pass the buck, to pass the problem on to someone else and thereby forget all about it. In this sense of 'refer', the tutor should never refer, since he should never completely hand a problem on to someone else. The student will not cease to be his tutee just because he has felt that he is not suitably equipped to handle a particular circumstance.

What he may need to do is ask for help or advice, and sometimes the help may extend to other people actually taking action to help the student.

Disciplinary referrals

Before I go any further, I would like to dispose of the disciplinary referral, where the tutor feels that he needs support from someone else in reacting to the student's misbehaviour. This is, of course, perfectly acceptable, and indeed may be advisable in certain cases if the tutor feels that his relationship with his tutee will be damaged if he involves himself too closely in her punishment. Generally, in such circumstances, the appropriate relationship should be able to take this kind of strain, and the tutor does have a very important disciplinary function as the person to whom, ideally, the tutee is closest – and perhaps whose approval she is most concerned to maintain.

Typically, the tutor will involve someone further up the disciplinary hierarchy, such as his head of year/house, and the problem here is one of integrity: the tutor has to be aware that some members of staff may deal with the student in a way of which the tutor may disapprove. This consideration will be the main factor which will influence the choice of person to whom the referral is made, though the procedures for referral may be so laid down as to preclude an option. The tutor should consider the implications of referring a student to a member of staff whose approach will be, say, more punitive than his own. Is the tutor simply getting someone else to do his own dirty work and is this how the student will regard it? It is generally preferable to involve someone else whose approach is philosophically in tune with his own. He can then be open with his tutee, who can see the action taken as an extension of his tutoring.

There might seem to be some doubt as to why a tutor might wish to refer 'up' if the methods employed are his own. There are a number of possibilities. It may be a matter of the time needed to deal with the issue. It might be that the tutor wants to convey to the student that he is not alone in disapproving of a particular kind of behaviour: in a disciplinary situation two 'parents' are generally more effective than one. It may be that the head of year, say, has skills which the tutor wishes to exploit. It may be that she has a particularly strong relationship with the student concerned. It should not be taken that referral 'up' in such circumstances is a defeat or an admission of weakness or even that it signifies that the tutor is less effective than the member of staff to whom the referral is made. This need not be the case: teachers are generally more defensive than they need to be about their control skills, and it is important that they are prepared to support each other and ask for help as equal colleagues irrespective of hierarchical rank.

The other disciplinary circumstance may also involve this issue. This is one in which the tutor feels that the tutee is out of his control in some way. This is unfortunate but it does happen, and it is certainly a case where senior staff may need to be consulted. The best solution here will depend on the school.

Ideally, all staff in the school will feel secure enough to be able to seek help when it is required. Often, the best person to consult will be the tutor as the person who is closest to the student. In such a school, where senior teachers seek help from young tutors, there is no loss of face involved in such a referral, and tutors who seek help from senior staff will not be judged incompetent.

But in schools where discipline is seen as a trial of strength, and kudos is to be found in capacity to control the unruly mob, I doubt whether the best solution is to pass the case over. The senior member of staff may be effective as a disciplinarian, but for the student to feel that she can control her while her own tutor cannot will help neither her relationship with her tutor, nor her future capacity to discipline herself, and it will certainly not help the tutor: his self-respect may be damaged – and his prestige, too. Referral in that case must involve getting advice from senior staff, and as in all such situations the advice you get will depend on the approach of the person you ask. Once again, therefore, it is important to consult someone who works within the same ideological and ethical parameters as you do, so that you can act in a way which is in tune with your usual approach to students.

A trivial but common situation where the tutor may feel that a disciplinary referral is appropriate is where a student is persistently late for registration in spite of frequent reproval. He should have gone through something similar to the following with the student: 'This is a minimum requirement of the school: that you attend on time. I have asked you several times to be prompt but you continue to be late. Have you got any particular circumstances which are making it difficult for you to get in on time?' Of course, if there are circumstances which are causing the lateness then these need to be addressed. If there are not, the tutor may feel that he needs reinforcements, and may bring in the head of year, say.

She sees the student concerned. The interview can be low key: 'This is a minimum requirement of the school: that you attend on time. Your tutor tells me that he has asked you several times to be prompt but that you continue to be late. Have you got any particular circumstances which are making it difficult for you to get in on time? [This is a courtesy.] We have to record attendance and punctuality on your record and employers, trainers and colleges regard poor timekeeping as an important weakness.' There may follow a warning of some sort – of contact with parents, perhaps – and she will tell the student that she will be asking the tutor to keep her informed about her timekeeping.

If the head of year knows the student particularly well, she may employ a less formal approach and may be able to exploit past contacts. She should certainly be prepared to help the tutor maintain his own effectiveness: she might, for example, suggest to the student that she is letting down her tutor who has supported her (if that is the case).

Some pastoral heads ask the tutor what he wants said or done on referral, and the above might be an approach. There are tutors who refer up hoping that the senior staff member will terrorise the student into compliance. This is not a reasonable expectation, partly because it should not be assumed that others can do what you are unable to do yourself, and if you want to terrorise the student and can't then maybe no-one else will be able to; and partly because the pastoral head may well wish to maintain her relationship with the student just as you do. It is the use of a second person in itself which is generally effective, though sometimes a teacher who has particular charisma with a student can be exploited.

Many referrals are not disciplinary, and are to be made because the tutor regards himself as less well equipped either in skills, personal qualities or knowledge to work with the student himself.

Using your pastoral head

Ideally, the tutor needs to work closely with the pastoral head, and certainly it is essential to keep her constantly informed of all action that he is taking. Where a circumstance is unfamiliar to the tutor he should consult with her. In the interests of good relations, and indeed of pastoral care for staff, he should not consult with senior management and certainly not make an official referral outside the school until or unless he has first consulted with the pastoral head and gained her agreement.

Your head of year/house may be a valuable resource for any or all of three reasons. First, she may well have known the student concerned for longer than you have, and may know the parents and older siblings. Second, she is almost certainly going to be a more experienced teacher than you are and also more experienced in dealing with the kind of problem – whatever it is – that you are facing. Finally she *may* (though this is by no means something you can rely upon) have had special training for the pastoral post that she holds.

Referral to your pastoral head is therefore the first stage in any kind of referral, and should be undertaken as a matter of course. There is always the possibility that she will take the problem out of your hands immediately. Whether she does so will depend on her view of you and of her role within the pastoral system, and on what the normal procedures in the school are. You can, of course, argue that you should keep control of it, or more subtly that you should continue to be involved.

The pastoral head can be involved in a variety of ways. You can discuss with her the problem, the student and the family, so that you deepen and widen your knowledge of the situation, benefit from another involved and informed person's perspective and have someone to bounce your own view of the situation off. Second, she may be able to give you advice as to the interpersonal skills which you might employ in dealing with the student or with her parents. If she has had counsellor training, this may be particularly enlightening. Third, you may feel that her skills in this respect make it beneficial to the student and the situation that she sees the student herself, to listen to her view of the situation and perhaps to give counselling help. Fourth, her experience concerning the use of other helping agencies may be employed, either in discussing possible referral to, say, the social services department, or in using the pastoral head to carry out such a referral.

The educational psychologist

As with other outside agencies, the tutor is not advised to contact the educational psychologist without first discussing such action with the pastoral head. The educational psychologist is an educational adviser. She has a degree or other academic qualification in psychology. She is not a doctor and is therefore not a psychiatrist. This distinction is an important one to make when you are discussing possible referral with parents – as you will have to, since the school is not permitted to refer to the educational psychologist without the parents' permission. Parents – and indeed students – are often threatened by the idea that the referral is to a psychiatrist because of the stigma associated with mental illness. Clearly this stigma is unfortunate and needs to be attacked, and schools may well be one agency which can make a contribution in this respect. Our main task, however, is to find the appropriate advice or agency, and to put the parents' minds at rest that it is not only appropriate but also a perfectly normal course which need not give rise to any anxiety.

The education psychological service is, in common with other helping agencies, overworked and understaffed, and teachers need to be realistic in their expectations of it. Much of the help which the educational psychologist gives is through giving advice to teachers so that they can work more effectively with the students, rather than through actual referral. It is unrealistic to expect them to undertake supportive counselling, for instance, which is labour intensive but requires less specialised skills. There may be someone in your school who is able to provide this – though teachers also rarely have the time needed if it is to be supplied over a long period. If it is short-term, you should be able to supply it yourself, as long as your objectives are limited to supportive listening (see Chapter 5).

The educational psychologist can be brought in to help with both learning difficulties and behavioural problems. The background to most appeals to the educational psychologist in the last few years has been the Education Act 1981, which sets out a procedure to be employed when the school identifies a student as having special educational needs. In theory these students can range from those who have fallen behind the majority for whatever reason and who need to be given extra tuition and support to those who have much more serious difficulties. They would also include all kinds of physical and mental disability.

The educational psychologist would normally be involved long before the procedures set up by the 1981 Act are invoked, in suggesting approaches which might be employed within the existing resources of the school. The Act requires that when a student's needs do not fall within the capacities of what is provided as a matter of course by the school, the agencies who have some involvement with the student shall jointly prepare a statement of her needs. This is called a Multi-professional Assessment (MPA).

The parents of the student, who will have been consulted during whatever strategies the school has employed and who should have been involved in the decision to carry out an MPA, are informed by letter that this procedure is to be undertaken, and have the opportunity to comment in writing. They may need the support and advice of the school in doing so. The school, the educational psychologist herself, the family doctor, the school medical officer, a social worker (where appropriate), and so on, all fill in a detailed form in which they express their particular view of the needs of the student concerned. The MPAs are brought together as a draft statement of need, which is sent to the parents for comment. If the parents agree to the proposals expressed in the draft statement, they sign and return it and it becomes the student's statement of need. The procedure is known as 'statementing' and students who have gone through the procedure are sometimes (probably unfortunately) labelled as 'statemented children'.

How far the tutor will be involved in this procedure will depend, as always, on the extent to which the tutor is ascendant, but it is a procedure which involves all aspects of the child's life and the tutor ought to be a party to it. He may even instigate it, though of course he will do this in consultation with the pastoral head, and indeed the headteacher.

There are of course circumstances where an MPA is inappropriate, since the school is in a position to supply the need through its normal resources but requires advice about how to handle the particular situation. You may ask the educational psychologist to interview the student, perhaps after or before discussing her difficulties with you (or with your pastoral head). This may happen where it is the behaviour of the student which is causing concern. The word 'behaviour' among teachers has tended to be used to imply 'bad behaviour', but I am using the word simply to mean 'the way a student behaves'. It may indeed be that teachers are having difficulty controlling a particular student or inducing her to do what they want her to do. It may be that a student does not appear to relate easily to other students – perhaps is being bullied. A student may be finding it difficult to concentrate in lessons and the complaints of her teachers have resulted in the tutor seeking help.

Social services

It is a good thing generally to get to know individuals at the agencies from which you need help, but this is especially true with social services departments. There is a lack of understanding between teachers and social workers which dates back a long way and which is as prevalent on one side as it is on the other. Traditionally, the teacher is a tough and uncompromising disciplinarian whose only concern is with the success or otherwise of pupils in the classroom. Traditionally, the social worker is a bit of a softy, who takes the side of youngsters who have no right to any excuses and blames everything on family background. Both stereotypes have some foundation, but the present situation on both sides is really very different. What problems there are arise from the misconception which each side has about the other, which are based upon those stereotypes.

Social workers on the whole tend to think that teachers have little interest in young people beyond the classroom. They do not expect teachers to care about any aspect of the student apart from her academic progress. They expect schools to be punitive in outlook. They do not expect teachers to concern themselves with the student's home life. Some social workers do not want the teacher to invade this area anyway, seeing it as their territory and the teacher as an untrained meddler. This is a comparatively rare view, though: most social services departments are delighted to involve concerned teachers, recognising that it is the teacher who has the day-to-day contact with the student.

They see this value especially in identifying cases of risk – young people who are in danger in one way or another.

It is a slow business convincing social services that we are interested, however, and the most effective way is to make close personal contact with the social workers who are involved with the members of your tutor group. Again, you need to involve your pastoral head in this project, but if you are prepared to make the time to engage in it the benefits to the students and to the school are notable. It is also of value to the social services department.

One basic characteristic of social services is that the rules within which they work are much more clear cut than those within which teachers operate. On the whole, too, the field of operation is much more emotive and open to sensational exploitation by the press. The teacher needs to be aware, therefore, that once something has been reported to social services it may be taken entirely out of her hands. It is useful, therefore, to be able to discuss an issue on a personal level with someone you know than to have to deal on an official basis with a department.

Social services on the whole like to work with families. They see the problems of one member of a family as impossible to consider in isolation. Thus, though a social worker may be involved in the first instance because of the actions of one member of a family, the social worker is unlikely to restrict herself to working with that person. Generally, a student will have a particular social worker who is assigned to her. Some students resent their social workers; others become very attached to and dependent upon them. Social workers, like teachers, as well as being concerned about their clients, also have their own careers to consider, and one of the difficulties is that they can at little notice and sometimes after a relatively short time with a particular case be transferred elsewhere, so that a student has to begin to relate to a new social worker. At such times the tutor can form a useful bridge, partly by helping the student to cope with the change, and also by rapidly getting to know the new social worker and passing on relevant personal information of the kind which is not to be found on file.

Much prominence has been given to the issue of child abuse recently, but neither violence within the family nor sexual abuse is new. As far as the former is concerned, social services departments operate a child abuse register. This contains the names of those children whom social services regard as at risk of abuse. Most social services departments furnish schools – or at least headteachers – with the names of students who appear on the register, and schools have an obligation to inform social services if they have reason to believe that such a student is being abused, if, for example, she arrives at a PE lesson with bruises on her body. There is also some obligation to inform social services if *any* child attends school with unexplained injuries, but this should not be done lightly. On receiving such information, social services departments have a statutory obligation to act, which means that they visit the home to ask for an explanation of the injuries. It is possible to misinterpret what a student says about an injury, or for a student to dramatise what a parent has done, and a teacher may at best look foolish and at worst cause unnecessary problems in the home, not to mention losing the trust of a student. Nevertheless, schools do have access to the lives of young people in a way which no other agency has and this brings with it special responsibilities which must not be evaded.

Your local authority will have child abuse procedures which must be followed, but in practical terms, if you have reason to suspect that a student in your tutor group is being deliberately injured or neglected at home, you should not keep it to yourself. Discuss your suspicions with your pastoral head or headteacher. If you have made personal contact with a social worker whom you trust and whom you feel respects your judgement, discuss it with her. Except under the most extreme circumstances, do not report it direct to the social services department without consulting someone else.

Sexual abuse is a problem which the tutor is far more likely to come across now than even five years ago. This is not because it is more common, but because it is more likely to be reported and because children who report it are more likely to be taken seriously. The taboo on incest in our society has never been as effective as some have liked to believe, but the taboo on talking about it was strong, and it is an improvement that the subject is now in the open. It is worth making your students aware of the issue: there are children who grow up so used to abuse that they do not realise that it is unusual; there are far more who would like to tell someone what is happening to them but are unsure how it will be received. To create a climate in which they feel that they can bring the problem to you is to provide a real service to such children.

Social services have a very wide brief, and can give advice and support on a whole range of issues. It is worth consulting a social worker on almost any issue which has a family dimension. In the majority of cases, the parents will have to refer themselves in order to receive actual help. Many people are unhappy about social service involvement. This is entirely comprehensible: before you allow yourself to be frustrated by this attitude, ask yourself how *you* would feel about a social worker calling to help you with your family problems. The association with 'problem families' in inner city areas is very strong and no family is happy with that label. If you feel that a student and/or her family would be helped by social service involvement, you will have to sell them the idea. The most effective way is to personalise the department by mentioning a particular social worker by name and ensuring if at all possible that it is she who makes the first contact at least. If the parent can meet the social worker at home or perhaps at school, this is generally preferred to having to attend the social services department.

If you and your school have managed to convey that parents are welcome to come into school at any time, as I suggested in Chapter 2 should be the case, then you may find that parents will bring problems to you which are outside the widest brief which could be accepted as a teacher's. Parents may consult you about the behaviour of their children at home, for example. In the event of a bereavement or marital breakdown, a parent may visit the school out of an unfocused need for someone to talk to. While teachers simply do not have the time to take on this kind of task, if you genuinely want parents to feel that they can consult you freely, you should not discourage such contacts. It can come within your sphere of action to act as a clearing house for such needs, and you will be a most valuable resource to the parents of your tutees if you know where they can get the appropriate help.

The Educational Welfare Officer

It is a parent's legal responsibility to see that her children attend school. Parents failing to ensure that a child attends regularly, and being unable to supply a satisfactory explanation – illness is obviously the most usual – can be prosecuted.

The EWO, as the Educational Welfare Officer is known, is the professional descendant of the 'School Board Man' or 'School Bobby', and with this lineage it is not surprising that EWOs are keen to convey to parents, to schools, and to the public in general that they are a helping profession and that their brief is wider than the enforcement of compulsory education. The EWO is the correct person, for instance, to see about families whom you believe to be in financial difficulties. She is responsible for all kinds of grants to cover school expenses, such as clothing, school meals, sports equipment and so on. Some LEAs locate EWOs with social services departments and the liaison between the two agencies – even though the education welfare service is part of the education department – can be very close.

Realistically, however, most schools use the EWO most in connection with school attendance. Practices vary from area to area, but EWOs generally visit all schools within their area regularly and frequently. They either check all registers on each visit or consult with pastoral staff who can recommend detailed checks on particular students whose attendance is causing concern.

At what stage a school would wish to refer a student will depend on the school, but in general it is a good idea to try a range of other methods to achieve an improvement in a student's attendance before making a referral to the EWO. As with social workers, it is desirable and possible for the school to have an ongoing relationship with the EWO. Whether, bearing in mind the pressure of time upon the EWO, it is reasonable to expect her to liaise with each tutor is another matter. Except in extreme cases, this is probably one instance where the pastoral head will have to be used as a channel for communication.

Initially, in the event of concern over poor attendance, the tutor should ask the student concerned *privately* whether there is any particular reason why she has been absent so much recently. What counts as a satisfactory explanation will vary from student to student. Clearly, genuine and frequent ill health will, though you need to ask yourself – and perhaps also the parent – whether the illness is serious enough to warrant absence from school.

There are all sorts of absences which are clearly not admissible – and which come under the heading, for the students, of 'skiving'. These range from missing a lesson after registering (with which the EWO will be less involved usually), through missing the same day each week in order to avoid a particular lesson – perhaps a particualr teacher, to missing weeks on end because the student finds school unbearable in some way.

The reason why a student misses school is important to learn, and it may not be the first answer you get – indeed the student may not be clear herself why she doesn't want to attend. A student who misses an afternoon lesson with a group of friends once in her school career can be dealt with summarily: a straightforward *quid pro quo* of apologising to the teacher concerned and making up the work missed, perhaps in a detention after school, is appropriate.

But many 'unexplained absences' are not pranks, but the tip of an iceberg – representing alienation, disillusion, isolation, inadequacy, separation anxiety (fear of leaving home, often fear of leaving a parent), fear of a teacher, disorganisation, and so on, and the only way to end the absences is to deal with the cause.

The situation is more complicated if the parent is colluding in the absence, that is, when the parent either knows of the absence and does nothing to discourage it, is unable to discourage it or perhaps covers up for the absence by inventing an excuse for the school's benefit, or where the parent takes the student somewhere – shopping, or the hairdresser, say – and gives that as the reason for the absence. This last type of case is very difficult, since dealing with it will involve telling the parent that your view is that the reason given for absence is not a sufficient one, and is a case where you would be well advised to refer the matter to your pastoral head (who might refer it to the headteacher), unless you have a very good relationship with the parent concerned. The other cases depend upon whether it is that the parent needs support in dealing with the student or that the collusion is willing. In the latter case, it is important to establish beyond doubt that the parent is willingly colluding. Students sometimes say, 'My mum knows,' when the parent will say something very different: sometimes the child is trying to play school off against parent and sometimes the parent is colluding and then lying about it.

It is in circumstances where the school is certain that the parent is aware of the absence but is not making much effort to deal with it (anything from encouraging the absence to being ineffectual in preventing it) that the EWO may be effective and should certainly be informed. Indeed, the school should keep the EWO informed of all cases causing concern even if they are not to be referred.

It needs to be accepted that few parents are delighted to receive a call from the EWO. It can be damaging to the school's relationship with the parent, therefore, to refer a student to the EWO without first speaking to the parent yourself about the absence. If the situation warrants it, you could explain the procedure which results in prosecution, namely a warning from the education department, followed by a three month period during which a check of the student's attendance is kept. If the check reveals a sufficiently serious problem, the parents are prosecuted, and have to attend court.

There are some kinds of absence which are technically illegal but where the school may feel unwilling to take action. A large family where the only parent has to go out to work may sometimes keep an older child at home to look after the younger ones. In the event of family illness, a child's help may be sought. During certain seasons, the unpredictability of the English weather may mean that a farming child is needed to help complete some urgent job – harvesting, for instance. None of these is always justified, but on occasions all could be acceptable reasons for absence. A school which works closely with the EWO will be able to discuss such cases with her.

Child Guidance

The service which is known as 'Child Guidance' is a complex organisation, its various workers employed by different agencies: the social workers by social services, the psychiatrists by the area health authority and the educational psychologists by the local education authority, though in some parts of the country the educational psychologists are less closely involved than in others. In fact, the operation of this cluster of helping professionals varies considerably from area to area.

Strictly speaking, if a psychiatrist is to be involved, it is not within the school's remit to refer children to this service, and referrals are most commonly through the family doctor of the child concerned. Nevertheless, it is possible for a school – with the agreement of the parents, of course – to make referrals, if what is required is therapy with a Child and Family Therapy social worker.

Like social services, the practice in Child Guidance is frequently to involve the whole family, and a considerable commitment is often required from all family members. Typically, such referrals would be appropriate in the case of persistent behaviour problems, such as school refusal, thieving, bullying and so on. Child Guidance uses psychiatrists (that is, doctors with qualifications in psychiatric medicine) and psychiatric social workers, and the therapy may be time-consuming.

The probation officer

Unlike Social Services, which is a department of local government, the probation service is run by the Home Office directly, though 50 per cent of its funding is provided by the local authority.

Since the Children and Young Persons Act 1969, young people under the age of 17 have not been put on probation but have in similar circumstances been subject to a Supervision Order. This supervision is generally the task of a social worker up to the age of 14, and of a probation officer above that age. In practice, however, the situation is more flexible, since if the family of the young person already has contact with a social worker, or if a member of that family already has a probation officer, that worker will often take over the young person as well, irrespective of her age.

Very shortly, the age up to which a social worker will have responsibility for the supervision order is to be increased to 16, though the same flexibility will be maintained. Nevertheless, this does reduce even further the extent to which schools will be in contact with the probation service.

The medical GP

Family doctors vary in their attitudes to schools and teachers, but generally once you have proved your genuine concern they can be most valuable contacts. I have known GPs who have treated teachers as fellow professionals (and why not?) and others who have been unco-operative.

Teachers need to understand first that the relationship between a doctor and her patient is a confidential one, and a doctor will need very good reason to discuss any aspect of a patient's health with a third person, however concerned. After all, there is doubt now whether even a parent has the right to be involved in her teenage offspring's medical care: since the Gillick judgment was overturned, GPs are able to prescribe the contraceptive pill to a person under 16 without informing the parents.

I have been able to discuss with their respective GPs the putative psychiatric condition of a school refuser and the physical injuries sustained by a student on the child abuse register. Often it is in the interests of the patient – and perceived by the GP to be so – that such a discussion take place, since the tutor may be able to throw light on the case. Teachers cannot expect necessarily to receive as much information from a GP as they are able to give to her. It would be petty to avoid a contact on those grounds, however, particularly if it was to the benefit of the student.

Many schools have a regular contact with their own school doctor. This clearly has some advantages in that the school doctor will be able to get to know some of the staff and is likely to be able and willing to pass on sensitive information where necessary. The problem is that a close relationship with a school doctor can actually make contact between the school and the GPs who attend the families of school children more difficult than it would otherwise be, and a special effort may have to be made to ensure that GPs are aware of channels of communication with the school.

The police

Most staff involved in pastoral care will sooner or later have some contact with the police. The most common situation is one where the police contact the headteacher for advice as to whether to prosecute a young person or not. What they usually want to know is whether the offence is a 'one-off' or an instance of characteristic behaviour, and to what extent a formal warning would be effective. This is a situation in which the tutor's opinion is valuable and should be consulted.

A formal warning is given where the person has not been suspected of an offence previously and is admitting the current offence. She has to attend the nearest main police station with a parent and is formally warned by a senior police officer what action will be taken in the future should she be apprehended again. Clearly, while many young people find the disgrace mortifying and the warning serves as a salutary shock, other young people imagine that a warning is equivalent to being let off.

In areas where there is a community police officer (a local 'bobby-on-the-beat'), there is considerable advantage to be gained from building a personal contact with her, particularly if some of your tutees are on the fringes of juvenile crime. The community police officer can be a valuable source of information concerning some of your tutees' out-of-school activities.

SELF-EXPLORATION

Each of the situations outlined below are cases which might confront any tutor who takes the care of his students seriously. Answer the following questions about each case:

1. What further information would you find useful?
2. Who would you like to talk to and in what order?
3. What other people or agencies would you refer to?
4. What outcomes would you be hoping for?
5. What might you do further yourself?

Debbie (aged 14): Mother has approached the tutor with her problem. She presents the child as untrustworthy and says she steals and lies constantly. She has no idea where she is when she's out or whether things she comes back with are come by honestly or not. She is willing for a referral to be made to anyone who could offer help, though she is suspicious and sceptical.

Daisy (aged 15): Student approached the tutor because she thought she was pregnant. She has now returned to report that she isn't. Nevertheless she could have been. It now transpires that the 'boy' concerned is 31.

Kevin (aged 15): Moved to the area to live with his father having previously fallen out with his mother who lives elsewhere. Now he has quarrelled with his father and has left home, alleging that his father has been hitting him. He rings the tutor late at night saying that he has 'run away'.

Jane (aged 15): Comes to see her tutor and reports offhandedly that her father has kicked her that morning. She shows the tutor a bruise on her thigh.

Carol (aged 13): Tutor sees her working in a cafe very late one evening (the employer is breaking the law on at least two counts; she is under 14, and so should not be employed at all; she is working outside the hours when even a 14-year-old could work).

Brian (aged 15): Has been in court for attacking another student outside schooltime. Having been a more or less model student up till that incident, Brian is now showing other signs of aggression in school. Two of his brothers have had custodial sentences for offences, and the family have a social worker because one of them is still on a supervision order.

Paul (aged 13): Sister (aged 15) has recently found that she is pregnant, to fury of parents. Paul reported to school as in possible danger of NAI, though is not on register. He arrives at registration with a black eye.

Bill (aged 14): You are informed by Social Services that his father has been arrested for sexually abusing Bill's elder brother.

Helen (aged 14): Mother rings to say that Helen has been absent on the previous afternoon because of a dental appointment. But Helen has already admitted, after fairly intensive questioning, that she 'skived'.

Chapter 5
Counselling Skills for the Tutor

Introduction

Since the prime task of the ascendant tutor is to develop a close and supportive relationship with his tutees, skills which are related to one-to-one helpful listening are among the most central. However, it is important to recognise, first, the limitations on the extent to which such skills can be conveyed in a book, and second, the level of counselling which it is possible, necessary and indeed desirable for a teacher in a secondary school to attempt.

On the first point, counsellors are generally trained over a period of at least a year. Much of this time is spent in developing the trainee's understanding of herself. Partly, this concerns how she appears to others, specifically to the client in a counselling interview, and partly, opportunities are provided for the trainee to develop an awareness of her own feelings. This training is not undertaken through lectures or reading but through putting trainees into a range of experiences in which they can give and receive information ('feedback') about how they appear, and discuss their feelings. This kind of thinking has to become habitual, to be 'internalised', and cannot just be tacked on as knowledge.

With regard to the second point, the shortage of time which is available to teachers to engage in one-to-one interviewing as well as the many other demands which teachers have to fulfil means that it is rarely possible for the tutor to undertake much more than helpful listening. The complexities of psychotherapy require someone with a lot more time both for the counselling process and to develop the skills and understanding necessary than teachers are on the whole able to find. From time to time, we may be able to offer a student an hour, but it is much more common for us to have to deal with a sensitive issue in five minutes.

There are other characteristics of the teacher's situation which differ from those of the counsellor in other spheres. As we shall see, teachers have a complex of different agendas – that is, a variety of different aims which they are trying to achieve. The tutor will be concerned that the outcome of whatever time he has invested with a student does at least not threaten order in the school and will not result in parental complaints, as well as wishing the student to gain from it. In 'proper' counselling, the agenda is exactly whatever the client want it to be.

Third, counselling only genuinely takes place when the client asks for it. In schools there are many occasions when a teacher wants to offer help but when it may not be actively sought by a student. A tutor may in some cases even feel that he should persuade a student to accept an opportunity to talk to him about some problem. That is not to say that one should ever pry into a student's affairs against her will: even if that were possible, the teacher has no right to do so. But a student may not actively seek help not because she doesn't want it but because it hasn't actually occurred to her that the tutor may be able to offer such a facility, and in such circumstances the tutor may feel that he should suggest it to her.

This chapter will therefore aim to give the tutor an idea of what kind of activity counselling is, so that he can begin to develop the skills which are appropriate to it – and indeed may seek further training if he wishes. It will also aim to improve the ability of the tutor to listen one-to-one and to help his tutee to talk freely and openly about a problem. To this end, some activities which should provide some practical starting points are included.

Focusing on feelings

Characteristically, the raw material or subject-matter of counsellor-listening is the feelings of the client. We are less concerned with thoughts or ideas: intellectualising is a distraction and may be a way of avoiding facing unpalatable truths. The feelings which are important are those which the client is having *now*, not those which she had yesterday or last week or last year.

A key question is therefore: 'What do you feel about ...?' The answer to this kind of question usually contains a feeling-word, such as 'worried' or 'sad', immediately after the word 'feel'. Thus, 'I feel anxious about it' is an authentic feeling sentence. It needs to be noted that sometimes the word 'feel' is used in English as an alternative for 'think' and sentences which begin 'I feel that ...' may not always be authentic expressions of feelings – though they may be: 'I feel that he doesn't like me' certainly could be.

Most people are not used to talking about their feelings and may resist it, so part of the counsellor's job is to keep the client within this kind of discourse. That means that the counsellor needs to be clear about what are feelings and what is really theorising. Intelligent adults sometimes analyse their feelings. This is not the same as expressing them, which is what the client needs to be doing, and the counsellor needs to be aware when that is happening and not join in with it. Asking and answering questions about why you feel something often comes into this category. Apart from being an intellectual activity, it frequently results in the client finding reasons for her behaviour outside herself, which has the effect of taking responsibility and power away from her, when the counsellor really wants the client to feel that she has control over her own life. For instance: 'I'm afraid of him because he treats me like my father used to' may be a way of saying 'I can't do anything about it'.

This brings me to the second point which needs to be stressed: counselling, though the word has the suggestion of giving advice, is not actually concerned with providing the client with answers or solutions. The temptation as a teacher is to do this, for, though most recent developments in learning approaches involve students finding out for themselves or using their peers as a resource, the notion that the teacher is a fount of knowledge and wisdom dies hard.

Actually, far from being a constraint on counsellor activity, the recognition that he is not expected to provide answers can be a relief, since the predominant feeling which teachers have when faced with sensitive and significant problems in the life of their students is often one of inadequacy. To provide an answer to a problem expressed by a student, even when the problem is expressed as a question, is a bad idea. To begin with, the tutor needs to understand fully how the student sees the problem, and until he does he is not in a position to make any suggestions (more about this later). Second, for the tutor to give answers is to take the responsibility on himself, and that means that if the course of action which he recommends turns out to be inappropriate or unsuccessful, he carries the blame. More seriously, because it is taking responsibility away from her, the client loses a sense of being in control of her own life. This may set a pattern which can recur when she has problems in future, so that she may tend to try to find other people who will take decisions for her. Finally, when he gives advice, he may be suggesting that would be right for him, and it may not be right for another person.

Counsellor presentation

When Truax and Carkhuff (1967) investigated the relative success of different schools of counselling and psychotherapy, the result appeared uninteresting at first: whichever approach was employed, the success rate seemed to be about 60 per cent. However, when they came to look at the personal qualities of individual counsellors, some striking correlations emerged. It seemed that a higher proportion of successful outcomes occurred when the counsellor exhibited three particular qualities in the counselling situation. The qualities were identified as empathy, congruence and unconditional positive regard.

It is worth spending a little time expanding on these concepts, not only because of the effect they can have in establishing a creative counselling relationship, but because, as Aspy and Roebuck (1977) argue, they are also qualities which benefit the teacher-student relationship and assist learning (and indeed contribute to good human relations in any sphere of activity). I have called them qualities, but it should not be thought that they cannot be learnt or developed.

Empathy is understanding how the client perceives the problem, seeing the world from the client's point of view. As Atticus Finch advises his daughter in Harper Lee's *To Kill a Mockingbird*, in order to understand another person, one should try to climb into her skin and walk about in it.

Empathy is not feeling the client's feelings, however, but understanding them. It is of little use if the counsellor feels the problem as the client does, for then he is in the same box as the client, and may, like the client, be unable to see beyond it. Thus, it is not necessarily a sign of good counsellor behaviour if the counsellor cries with the client. Though it may happen and may be understandable, it is not, as is sometimes thought, to be desired. Indeed, it may happen if, because of some experience of his own, the counsellor identifies too closely with a problem. This is undesirable, because he may be unable to make the distinction and see the inevitable differences between his own situation and the client's, as well as because he may be trapped by the same constraints as she is.

Congruence is being oneself. If the counsellor is congruent, all the aspects of his behaviour are consistent. His words are congruent with his tone of voice, his posture, gesture and facial expression all give the same messages. An alternative which is often used is genuineness, but a more expressive term is openness. The suggestion is that only when someone is being open or genuine about her feelings do all the signals which convey what she feels cohere.

Teachers sometimes find this quality difficult to learn. Traditionally, they have tended to withdraw behind a 'teacherish' exterior particularly when they have felt threatened. Congruence is epitomised by a willingness to admit to weakness and failure, while teachers often feel that they should maintain an invulnerable exterior. In a counselling relationship – and indeed I would argue in any real relationship – it is necessary to reveal vulnerabilities. Doing so permits the client to reveal her own, as well as making trust more likely, since she will feel that the counsellor whom she is experiencing is the real person, rather than a professional façade. The opposite of congruence is phoniness.

Unconditional positive regard is a transatlantic mouthful, but is actually more informative than its more British counterparts, warmth or acceptance. Positive regard is the attitude of the counsellor that the other person has the right to be herself, that she has value. It is different from liking, since it does not depend upon the qualities which the counsellor finds in the client. This is what makes the regard unconditional, since the client should have the feeling that the positive regard will not be withdrawn no matter what she says or does, no matter what she reveals about herself. In this respect it is more akin to some kinds of loving than it is to liking.

In a climate of unconditional positive regard, the client will feel that she will not be judged by the counsellor, so this aspect of counsellor behaviour is sometimes called 'being non-judgemental'. The client can feel safe that she can say whatever she is feeling or thinking, so that she is virtually able to think aloud. This is clearly what is required in a counselling situation.

The opposite of unconditional positive regard is a 'shock-horror' reaction after some disclosure. The difficulty for teachers is that they may feel inclined to react with disapproval where the client is a student who has acted in a way of which society, the student's parents, or the school authorities would disapprove. Indeed, some teachers may feel a responsibility to react in this way.

In a counsellor, such a reaction is unhelpful, and it must be taken into consideration that many students would be unlikely to feel able to talk freely to a teacher whom they think may react in this way. Indeed, it is the capacity of the teacher to be non-judgemental which makes him a more likely recipient of confidences than the student's parent, since while the parent has an emotional axe to grind in the behaviour of her offspring, a teacher, though concerned, can be less involved.

In a sense, congruence and unconditional positive regard are in conflict since to be non-judgemental may involve the tutor in suppressing a wish to express his own strong beliefs, and if he is suppressing anything of himself then he is not being congruent. Part of the answer to this is to say that in a counselling session the counsellor's views are an irrelevancy and the counsellor should not seek to push himself with all his quirks, opinions and personal values at the client, whose time it is. But that is not to say that the counsellor has to pretend that he does not hold such views. Also, it is necessary to distinguish between the act, of which one may disapprove, and the agent. I can disapprove of an action perpetrated by one of my students without making the student feel that I disapprove of or reject her.

In order to focus upon the specific points of behaviour which can encourage disclosure, it may be useful to consider behaviour which is offputting in a listener. This can be divided into three categories: postural, facial and verbal.

POSTURAL

The first general rule is that posture should not constitute a distraction. Fidgeting or fiddling with anything, frequent shifting of position, hand or arm movements are all to be avoided if possible.

Second, the posture of the counsellor should be encouraging and welcoming, and should never give the impression that he would rather be doing something else. An open posture, that is one without arms or legs crossed is generally felt to be best; crossing limbs can feel like a barrier. Sitting behind a desk is certainly setting a barrier between counsellor and client.

Third, the counsellor should convey that he is attending, so he needs to be looking in the general direction of the client. Having his back to the client at any point while listening is generally inappropriate. If the counsellor leans too far back in his chair, it can suggest lack of interest or concern to the client. The epitome of unhelpful listening behaviour is when the counsellor looks at something else sporadically, implying that only part of his attention is engaged. Peering at someone else behind the client is very disconcerting. Looking at his watch, especially if this is done covertly, is at least as bad. Most counsellors work to a tight time schedule; teachers counselling in school must do so inevitably. But it is better to explain the time constraints at the beginning of the interview, and have the watch or clock on clear view to both client and counsellor, than to give the impression that the counsellor is getting bored. Yawning is similar: if the counsellor has to yawn, it is better to do it openly and apologise, than to try to cover it up.

Fourthly, the counsellor's posture should not intimidate the client.

Leaning too far forward can have this effect, as can sitting too near to the client. It is also generally felt preferable to sit at right-angles to the client, rather than full-frontally which suggests confrontation. The most effective way to intimidate the client, as most teachers will know, is to conduct the interview from a greater height. The traditional model for the teacher-student (or here 'pupil' might be more apt) conversation is for the teacher and pupil to stand, so that the teacher, who is usually taller than the student, is able to look down upon her – in every sense. This is quite inappropriate in a counselling interview (the tutor may feel that it is quite inappropriate for any teacher-student interchange). It is often worth deliberately seating the client in a chair which is higher than that of the counsellor.

There is sometimes something to be gained in mirroring the client's own posture, though clearly this should not be overdone. But sitting as the client does can convey empathy. Friends often do this quite unconsciously when talking comfortably together.

FACIAL

As I have said, the counsellor needs to face in the general direction of the client all the time. Eye-contact is often felt to be essential, but it should be remembered that eye-contact can actually be intimidating, and should not be overdone. If the counsellor stares fixedly at the client's eyes, particularly if he is leaning forward, the effect can be quite inhibiting. It is generally better to watch the area around the mouth and/or nose.

Facial expression needs to match the mood of the client's discourse. It can be very disconcerting if the client is expressing feelings of sorrow and the counsellor is smiling – or indeed vice versa. It is an indicator of lack of attention. However, there are times when the client herself will smile or frown inappropriately. Some people smile even when relating the most distressing situations. Others will frown self-deprecatingly when speaking of their own achievements. So it is not always the case that the counsellor's facial expression should mirror that of the client. It is the feeling that is being expressed which to which he should respond.

VERBAL

If someone has something very important, perhaps sensitive, to say, maybe even something which she finds difficult to share with someone else, she will need to feel that she does not have to fight to get a word in edgeways. This sense that the counsellor is giving the client time to express what needs expressing is what counsellors sometimes rather paradoxically call 'giving space'. Anything which closes down this space will inhibit the client's disclosure.

The most obvious example of this is interrupting. If the counsellor cuts in when the client is talking, she will feel that she is competing for talking time. This is the case even if the counsellor cuts in with a supplementary question or a supportive comment.

It is far worse, however, if the counsellor cuts in to 'take over the problem', by saying something like 'Oh yes. I've had just that feeling. I remember a few years ago ...' and goes on to talk about himself. The implication is that the counsellor is not terribly interested in the client's problem: he is much more interested in himself.

It is actually rarely helpful, though many people think it will be, for the counsellor to say that he has had the same experience or that lots of people do. The effect is to devalue the client's experience, to suggest that the client 'ought' not to be so worried about it as it is so common. It is also to *judge* the client.

Being judgemental is always inhibiting to the client. To say, for example, 'Oh, you shouldn't have done that' is clearly unhelpful. Less obviously, it is not generally a good idea to ask questions beginning 'Why ...?' To be asked why is often felt by the client to be challenging what she has done, which is a form of judgement. If the counsellor wishes to understand the client's motivation, a less judgemental form of words might be 'What were you feelings when you did that?'. 'What is it about that situation that makes you feel that?' is preferable to 'Why do you feel that?' for a similar reason. 'Why do you feel that?' carries the implication that to feel that is stupid or unnecessary or wrong.

Even giving favourable opinions may not be as helpful as it might seem, since any opinion suggests that the counsellor is evaluating the client's behaviour. It also suggests that the counsellor has some firm idea of what the 'right' behaviour should be. 'Stroking' – the making of encouraging remarks or gestures or even noises – can be valuable in suggesting empathy but is better if it is related to what the client is pleased about, rather than if it expresses the counsellor's opinion.

Prompts

The rules of normal conversation are very different from the rules of the counselling interview. Normal conversation is similar to tennis: mostly, we take it in turns. First, you say a bit and then you stop and I say a bit and then I stop and this is the signal for you to have your turn again – and so on. The rules of the counselling interview are that the client should do all the talking and the counsellor all the listening – at least until the counsellor and client have both explored the nature of the problem fully. Any counsellor behaviour which limits the extent to which the client talks is, as we have seen above, unhelpful.

However, while the counsellor is aware of the rules of the counselling interview, the client is not, and she continues to operate within the conventions of normal conversation. The methods by which the counsellor employs the conventions of normal conversation in order to achieve a situation where the client does most of the talking are known as prompts.

Basically, the counsellor needs to use a prompt when the client stops as she would in normal conversation to let the counsellor have his turn at speaking. The counsellor needs to 'put the ball back in the client's court', to make her feel that it is her turn to speak again, and he needs to do this without saying very much. If he can, at the same time as conveying that he does not want a 'turn', also convey that he has heard and understood what the client has said, so much the better.

First, there are minimal prompts. Examples of these are when the counsellor says 'yes' or 'mm', or grunts, or nods when the client looks at him. These may or may not be effective as prompts – it depends how freely the client is talking – though they do tend to make the client feel that the counsellor is listening. They can become irritating, however, if they are overdone.

Second, when the client stops, the counsellor can say 'Can you tell me some more about that?' This is not very subtle, but it follows the rules of normal conversation and can be very effective in eliciting a response.

Thirdly, it is possible for the counsellor simply to say nothing when the client stops. The ensuing silence will convey to the client that the counsellor does not wish to leap in as would frequently be the pattern in normal conversation. This gives her a sense of the 'space' which he is making available to her. For many people, silence in conversation is difficult and they will feel pressure to fill it. Though this sounds a little brutal, the counsellor can use this pressure – as long as he feels comfortable in the silence – to put the onus of speech back on the client.

It is a good idea to develop the capacity to feel comfortable in silence. Most people are able to sit in silence with someone. Next time you are sitting in silence with that person, be aware of the ease that you feel. When you find yourself in a situation were there is a silence which is less comfortable, imagine you are back with your friend and concentrate on that feeling.

The fourth approach to prompting is the one which counsellors use perhaps more than any other. This is known as 'reflecting back'. In effect, the counsellor repeats back to the client what she has just said. He can do this either in more or less her words, known as 'parroting', or in his own as a paraphase.

The value of reflecting back is that it not only complies with the rules of normal conversation by constituting the counsellor's 'turn' at speaking, and thereby passes the onus to speak back to the client; it does this without the counsellor having distracted from the client's discourse by adding anything of his own; it lets the client know that her words have been heard and taken in: and in the case of paraphrase it is a means for the counsellor to check that he has understood what she has said, since she has an opportunity to confirm or otherwise that the paraphrase is accurate.

SELF-EXPLORATION
Consider the following examples of student self-disclosure:

1. I'm feeling really low at the moment. I don't have any friends at all. Nobody seems to like me. I have to do everything on my own. Nobody ever asks me to join in with them. I even have to sit by myself in lessons. I try to be nice to people but it doesn't seem to make any difference. It's the same at home too. Nobody wants to have anything to do with me.

2. I'm feeling much happier now. I'm doing quite well at school, and my parents are really pleased with me. I've got to know some nice people in my class too, and I've been made school council rep. Most of my teachers have said I'm doing well. Everything seems to be going really well.

3. My parents don't really like me much. My sister gets all their attention. They're always going on about how wonderful she is; all I get is criticism. I get blamed for everything too – even when it's her fault. I dont know what I can do.

4. I've had enough of school. I'm fed up of being pushed around by the teachers. You always have to do what they say even when it's a total waste of time. Nothing we do has anything to do with what I'm going to do when I get out of here. I've had enough of being treated like a little kid. I'd like to see the whole lot go up in flames.

5. I can't stand anyone here. Everyone calls me names. They call me 'Fatso' and laugh at me, and if I hit them they go and tell a teacher, so I get into trouble for bullying. All I'm doing is sticking up for myself. I'm not standing for it, though. They'll be sorry, you see.

6. I've never been able to get anywhere in school. It's not that I don't try: I do.

But I just seem to do it all wrong. I'm never sure what the teachers want. Sometimes I think I know and then when I get the work back I find I didn't after all. Everyone seems to do better than me and they all laugh at me when I make mistakes in class. I just feel stupid all the time.

Assume that each of the above paragraphs is the first statement made in a counselling session by one of your tutees.

What should be your next response? Remember, the intention is to encourage further exploration of the problem and to help the student to feel that you are following and understanding what she is saying. Avoid saying anything which looks like an answer or solution.

When you have written your response for each, consider the following responses. Are any similar to yours? Do you think that any are better than yours? Which do you think are poor responses and why?

1 (a) Whatever you do, you mustn't give up. If you persevere in your efforts to get to know people, you're bound to make friends eventually.

  (b) I'm sorry you're so unhappy. You keep trying to make friends but nothing you do seems to work. You're beginning to think there's something wrong with you.

  (c) When you say you try to be nice to people, what do you actually do?

  (d) You're feeling really bad at the moment because nobody seems to like you.

2 (a) I'm pleased you've been made school council rep. What we need to do now is think about what else you can do so that things will stay good for you.

  (b) You're feeling really excited because things are going so well.

  (c) Well, I don't think this mood is going to last for very long.

  (d) I'm glad to hear everything is going so well for you. I can see how excited you are. Other people are pleased with you and you enjoy pleasing them.

3 (a) You seem to be really angry and desperate about the situation at home. You don't feel as if you're valued and you can't see any way of improving things.

  (b) You're feeling that your parents don't really like you. They seem to value your sister rather than you and it's making you really unhappy.

  (c) Have you discussed your feelings with your parents? It's quite likely they've no idea how bad you're feeling and it's a good idea to get it out in the open.

  (d) You're just getting depressed. Of course your parents love you. There's no need to be jealous of your sister; what you need to do is to make an effort to make your parents pleased with you.

4 (a) You're obviously very angry. You can't see the point of what you're asked to do in school and you don't like the lack of freedom.

  (b) Let's have a look at the subjects you're taking and see whether there's any value you can get out of them.

  (c) You're bound to find some things more useful than others in school. The teachers are all trying to find things which will be interesting. What you have to do is do your best, and I'm sure things will work out fine for you.

  (d) So you're thinking about burning the school down. You must be very angry. It seems to be because you don't like being told what to do all the time.

5 (a) Have you ever thought that it may be because you go round hitting smaller boys that people call you names?

  (b) You're a big, strong lad but people only make fun of you. When you try to get your own back, you get punished for bullying. You're feeling very unhappy and lonely.

  (c) You must be careful. Nobody likes a bully and all you'll do is get into more trouble.

  (d) You're feeling very angry. You've had enough of people being nasty to you and you're going to do something about it.

6 (a) Even though you're really making an effort, nothing seems to go right, and it's making you very unhappy.

  (b) Don't get discouraged. If you're really doing your best, it's sure to produce results in the end.

  (c) Maybe you need to improve the way you organise your work. Let's have a look at how you study and see if we can see where you're going wrong.

  (d) You're feeling miserable. Even though you always try your hardest, nobody seems to appreciate you and you're afraid that I may turn out to be just the same as everyone else.

It would not be true to say that some of the responses suggested above are 'right' and some 'wrong'. In the field of relationships, things are rarely as simple as that. Nevertheless, there are some principles which may guide your evaluation of the responses you have suggested. A discussion of the alternatives given to the first client may illustrate these.

(a) Whatever you do, you musn't give up. If you persevere in your efforts to get to know people, you're bound to make friends eventually.

The opening sentence of this response is wholly directive: it is telling the client what she ought to do. There is no attempt to encourage the client to explore further the problem which she has come to talk about, in spite of the fact that the counsellor really knows relatively little at this stage.

Moreover, the advice the counsellor gives implies a judgement, namely, that the client is wrong to give up the strategies she has been using. He is telling her that she has not done all she could. But the counsellor has no idea what approach the client may use to other people which may be causing them to dislike or avoid her – so his assumption that all she has to do is persist is quite unjustified.

It is not only advice that is being given: the counsellor is trying to reassure the client, and though we may often feel we want to provide reassurance, it is often not a good idea since it tends to prevent the client from exploring the problem further. It is dishonest, too, since the counsellor is not in a position to assure the client that things will turn out all right in the end.

(b) *I'm sorry you're so unhappy. You keep trying to make friends but nothing you do seems to work. You're beginning to think there's something wrong with you.*

There is some warmth and sympathy in this response, and the reflecting back is accurate and helpful, since it shows that the counsellor has listened and understood what the client has been saying. The first two sentences might thus result in the client feeling encouraged to tell the counsellor more.

But the final sentence spoils the response. Not only is it adding an element which is not present in the client's disclosure, and one for which the counsellor has no real warrant, it is also a very negative addition. It may be true, of course, but if it is not, then to put this idea into the client's mind could be very destructive.

(c) *When you say you try to be nice to people, what do you actually do?*

This has one initial advantage: it is short. The counsellor doesn't want to talk himself, but to encourage the client to do so.

It is also a constructive line to take, since it is likely from what we know so far that something in the client's behaviour is putting people off her. But – and it is an important 'but' – we really don't know enough at this stage to be looking at solutions so soon. What the counsellor should be doing at this stage is showing that he has heard and understood what the client has said so far, and encouraging her to further explain and explore her perception of the problem. To look at what exactly the client may be doing wrong in her relationships may well be a good line to take – *later*.

(d) *You're feeling really bad at the moment because nobody seems to like you.*

This is an effective prompt. First, it reflects back not only a brief summary of the content of the disclosure, but also the feeling within it. The client will probably feel that the counsellor has understood the facts in general and also has emphathised with the feelings which she has.

As well as this, it is brief, and puts the ball quickly back into the client's court. If it has a flaw, it is that it is perhaps a little arid: but the counsellor could convey sympathy by his tone of voice.

Now analyse the responses you have suggested to Nos 2 – 6 in the same way.

Observing the client

Though in the previous section we have been concentrating on the words spoken by the client, it is far from being the case that words are the only data which the counsellor has available to him. As we saw earlier, the counsellor conveys a great deal to the client by the way he sits, his gestures and facial expression. The same is true of the client, and the counsellor needs to be watching as well as listening if he is to appreciate fully how the client is feeling.

Part of the function of congruence – openness – in the counsellor is to encourage the client to be open too. Realistically, though, we have to recognise that the client may very well not be at all aware of her own feelings: indeed, it is part of the counsellor's job to help her to be more aware of them. What she says may very well be at odds with the messages which the counsellor is able to pick up from her posture, movements and facial expression.

It is always important that the counsellor notices and notes the information which the client gives non-verbally. Sometimes, he should actually point it out to the client. For instance, there may be a value in pointing out to the client that, though she says she is relaxed and happy, while she has been talking she has been pulling at the skin around her finger nails. Or to suggest that, while the client expresses her sorrow at what she has done, she appears cheerful and animated.

It is not always a good idea to point it out to the client like this, because it is in a sense a rejection of what she says she is feeling: if it is pointed out, it must be done gently and as a mere statement of fact rather than as a challenge.

There are other times when pointing out what you have noted in the client's non-verbal behaviour may be used to confirm her words. The counsellor may be able to say, 'Yes, I can see how much happier you are from the way you're sitting. It's very different from how you sat here last week.' This kind of more objective confirmation of what she is feeling can be valuable for the client, and that applies when the feelings are negative as well as positive.

Sometimes, it is possible for the counsellor to discern when the client is appproaching an area of her disclosure which is particularly important to her. She may reveal anxiety or strength of emotion, for instance, and such bodily indications may lead the counsellor to encourage her to explore this particular area more thoroughly. Some people, half-conscious that their bodies may betray them, may try to control them so that they cannot. People who are afraid of saying too much in gesture may sit on their hands. People who fear that the tears in their eyes may be spotted may look away from the counsellor. Again, the counsellor may feel that he should draw the client's attention to what he has spotted, or he may pursue a particular line without saying why he is doing so – or he may just store it away in his mind for future reference.

Counselling in school

There are certain aspects of the school setting which alter the kind of task which counselling is for the teacher. Some of these are positive and make the job of the tutor qua counsellor easier. Others make it more difficult.

ROLE CONFLICT

Teachers have to fulfil a variety of different functions in schools. As well as subject teachers and counsellors, they are also administrators, managers, social organisers, policemen, detectives, judges, crowd controllers, public speakers, social workers, public relations officers, surrogate parents, older siblings, prison warders, hangmen (though not literally!), and many more. In time, most teachers develop the capacity to handle these different demands, and students learn to manage the shifts from one to the other too.

However, to reconcile the authority role which teachers inevitably have with the counselling function is less easy than most, and deserves particular consideration.

The counsellor's prime task is to establish what the client wants to achieve and to help her to achieve it. The listening part of counselling is all aimed at finding out what the client regards as in need of change in her life. Once she has explored the problem with the help of the counsellor, she may often decide that understanding it in itself provides the solution. She may now be able to accept the aspect of her life which was unacceptable before. Or the solution to her problem may be apparent now that she understands the problem.

However, the client may decide that she does need to make changes in her life, and within a school context the direction she wishes to go may conflict with school rules, parental aspiration or even the prescriptions of society. To take an example, she may decide that she has no wish to continue struggling for high GCSE grades in order to become a doctor as in the past she has always wished – and as her parents wish. Now all she wants is to marry her boyfriend as soon as possible.

Now this is a direction which the school as an institution disapproves of, which the parents are dead against, which society will (if it can be said to have a coherent opinion on this subject) regard as a waste of talent, and which the tutor, whose counselling has produced this outcome, is also himself decidedly unhappy about. As an educator, he wants to encourage his students to raise not lower their aspirations. He is also conscious of the low success rate of teenage marriages. All in all, what he wants to do is to try to persuade his client to stay on at school and postpone or abandon her marriage plans. But as a counsellor, this is not part of his job.

Again, a client decides after counselling that what she really wants is not to come to school at all, that all her unhappiness stems from this. The tutor as counsellor is then in a position of colluding with actions which as member of the teaching staff and therefore of the control system in the school he has a responsibility to prevent – whether he approves of her decision or not.

These are clear-cut examples. Most are less so, but the teacher as counsellor will frequently feel that his agenda – that is, the objectives he sets for the counselling session – are not necessarily open-ended. He has certain demands and responsibilities, to the school, to parents, to society, which he cannot simply ignore. The tutor needs to be aware of these constraints, and openness demands that if he suspects that they are going to be relevant and to limit his capacity to be entirely non-directive he needs to make this clear to the client.

However, since, as I have suggested, the bulk of tutor counselling is confined to helpful listening, the issue of helping the client to achieve an objective – acceptable or otherwise – will frequently not arise. An issue which often does arise is that of confidentiality.

CONFIDENTIALITY

Legally, only the relationship between a lawyer and her client is confidential. That is, only a lawyer cannot be required in a court of law to reveal the substance of any conversation which took place between her and her client. However, in practice, because the Hippocratic Oath, the doctor's code, requires doctors to keep confidence with their patients, the medical profession are rarely expected to break it. Professional counsellors are in some cases doctors – probably psychiatrists – and this holds good for them too. The rest of the counselling profession take this medical model for their own guide and would resist attempts to coerce them into breaking client confidence.

Counsellors in schools, however, as we have seen in the previous section, have fairly clear cut responsibilities to other people than their clients. Moreover, many of their clients are under the age of sixteen and are thus not in a position legally to make even medical decisions for themselves. There would seem, therefore, to be good reasons for regarding confidentiality as irrelevant and impossible for the counsellor in school.

On the other hand, the same basic requirement for confidentiality which applies in other contexts applies in school, namely, that if the student believes that what he says may be passed on to anyone whom the teacher wishes to tell, she is unlikely to use him as a counsellor. It is thus desirable that students trust the tutor to keep confidentiality.

This dilemma is less intractable than might appear. It arises from the fact that we imagine that all kinds of situations might arise in which the tutor (or other teacher-counsellor) will feel he should pass on to a third person information which the client wishes him to keep to himself. Now in practice this rarely happens.

When a student approaches her tutor or another teacher for help with a problem, or when she accepts an offer of help, it is unusual for her to have any particular preconceptions about the kind of help which she is going to receive. She wants help and if the teacher has to involve other people, other teachers or other professionals, to assist in finding a solution she is unlikely to demur. On those occasions when she is seriously worried about information being passed on, it tends to be because she is unwilling that her parents should know whatever it is. She may also be concerned lest her problems become gossip-fodder in the staffroom.

Thus, if a student asks if you will keep confidential what she has to tell you, the question needs to be attended to seriously and it needs to be clarified just who it is she does not wish to be told. First, you need to make it clear that if there is any question of law-breaking, you may not be able to keep that to yourself. Second, you need to say that you may feel that other professionals need to be consulted. Third, you can reassure the student that you will not pass on anything to anyone who does not need to know – that is, you will not gossip about her. The two contentious areas are: will you have to tell her parents? and, if a question of breaking school rules is involved, will you have to take it further as a disciplinary issue? In my view, both of these are negotiable.

In the last few years, there have been moves towards recognising increasingly the rights of parents. Paradoxically, this move has taken place at a time when abuse of all kinds of children by their parents has come very much into the open. I do not believe that a parent's rights are inalienable. Indeed, they seem to me to be rights which a parent can very quickly forfeit if she shows herself to be putting her offspring in danger of any kind. Consequently, though we cannot assure a student that her parents will not be informed, there is no need to assure her that they will.

Teachers sometimes say: 'I'd want to know about that if she was a child of mine.' Certainly, a decision *not* to inform a parent about something important in a child's life should not be taken lightly. The teacher should have good reasons for any action which puts a barrier between parents and school, for as we have seen in Chapter 2 parents are a vital resource if the student is to be successful in school. Nevertheless, the assumption by a teacher that another parent would react to a problem involving her child as she would is naïve. Also, as the student gets older, her rights as an individual may be felt to increase. She is capable herself of making intelligent and mature decisions, in some cases perhaps more so than her parents.

In the end, too, the student is the client and the consumer of the service we have to provide, and our first responsibility is to her. We may fulfil this responsibility best by keeping parents fully informed but there are cases in which we do not.

As far as the school authorities are concerned, this too may be negotiable. Most teachers recognise that there may be times when a school offence is best not reported. If the student has approached the tutor for help, there may be more important factors to consider than whether a rule has been broken.

What is important, though, is that the tutor is open with the student about what level of confidentiality is being offered – if any. I have never known a student who refused to persist with a disclosure because I refused to promise that it would be kept confidential. Saying, 'I can't promise to keep it to myself until I know what it is', is entirely honest, and most students feel safer with that than with a too readily given promise.

Once the student has made the disclosure, it may be that the tutor needs to negotiate concerning who needs to be told. It is always preferable to have the student's permission to pass on information to a third person than to do it without, so it is worth spending some time explaining why a certain person needs to be informed, what she will do with the information, whether she will have to involve anyone else, and so on.

There are of course cases where the tutor feels that someone should be informed while the student does not consent. For instance, the tutor may feel that for his own protection he needs to inform the head teacher – to share the responsibility, in other words. If the information concerns an offence the student may not be happy about this. But it may actually be an opportunity for the head teacher to be shown to the student in a more sympathetic light. If you know the head teacher will react in a punitive way, this decision will be more difficult.

A case where the dilemma is more evident is one where a female student reveals that she thinks she is pregnant, but she is unwilling for her parents to be told. If she is pregnant, paradoxically it is more straightforward, since sooner or later her parents will have to know and most girls will see this. However, if she is mistaken, the problem is more difficult. Clearly, if she thought she was pregnant, then assuming she understands how conception occurs she could have been, and the tutor may feel that this is information which the parent ought to know. If the girl is under sixteen (so that the offence of sexual intercourse with a minor has been committed), the responsibility to pass this on may be felt to be even stronger. If the tutor has also discovered that the potential father is for instance over 30, then that may be another factor to strengthen his resolve to tell the student's parents. Yet they may be just the reasons which the student has for not wanting the information passed on.

Such cases need to be thought through, if possible before they occur. The following exercise is an opportunity for this kind of thinking.

SELF-EXPLORATION
Confidentiality
For each of the following student disclosures, think:

- What would I feel?
- What would I do immediately?
- What would I do in the longer term?
- How far would I be able to maintain confidentiality?

1. I think I'm pregnant.
2. My friend is sniffing butane gas.
3. David Smith went shop-lifting in Woolworths last week.
4. I don't like some of the things my dad asks me to do.
5. Sheila Banks took a crib-sheet into GCSE Physics yesterday.
6. My boyfriend is having sex with someone else because I won't.
7. My mum drinks whisky at breakfast time.
8. Peter's got awful bruises on his legs.

CHANGING THE STUDENT'S ENVIRONMENT

The counsellor in a non-school context will expect generally to be able to improve the client's situation only by helping the client to change it herself. But the teacher-counsellor is sometimes in a position to change the student's environment for her. For instance, he may be able directly to alter the behaviour of another student towards his client – to prevent bullying, perhaps. Or he may be able to arrange for his client to transfer to a different option or a different teaching group.

Another case where direct tutor intervention may be appropriate is where the tutor may wish to mediate between the student and another member of staff. It is often more effective to help the student to improve her own relationship with the teacher concerned, rather than to do it for her, but there are times where the tutor can, for example, prepare the ground for the student, perhaps where the student is intending to apologise to the teacher but where the tutor is unsure what kind of response she is likely to get.

While this capacity to intervene directly in the client's environment gives the teacher-counsellor an advantage in one way, it means that the temptation to intervene and so to take the responsibility away from the student may be harder to resist. Removing the student from a situation in which she is not coping well may be a solution to that problem, but it may set a pattern for the future whereby she may try to escape from problems rather than endeavouring to deal with them.

Also, sometimes changing the environment may be curing the symptoms but not the underlying causes. Thus, a student who is not coping in French may be transferred to Physics. This may appear to solve the problem, but subsequently the student may reappear with a similar difficulty in Physics: the move was just a way of evading responsibility, and in the long run the counsellor might have been better advised to help the student find ways of coping with French.

PRESENTING PROBLEMS

The 'presenting problem' is the reason which the client gives for coming to see the counsellor in the first place. Both doctors and counsellors find that often the presenting problem is not the one which is really the cause of concern, but that the real problem causes too much stress for the client to be able to mention it immediately. She needs to be able to come round to it as she relaxes.

For the teacher-counsellor, it is even more difficult, since students have lots of reasons for coming to see their tutor other than because they are seeking counselling. The tutor has to be on the alert, therefore, since even when a student appears for the most mundane or practical of reasons, it is always possible that there is some other and more sensitive reason for her visit. A student might arrive asking for a rough-book, for example. The clue is that when the tutor has handed the book over, the student does not seem keen to go. Part of the tutor's job which a counsellor never has to undertake is to encourage students to make themselves clients for counselling.

Counsellors can have a hard-and-fast rule: only counsel clients who *ask* to be counselled. For the teacher, it is more complicated. For one thing, students need to know that counselling is something which the tutor is able and willing to provide. Second, the tutor who takes responsibility for his tutees will be monitoring them (however informally). As a result, he may become aware that a tutee has a problem and want to offer help. Third, students are sometimes shy about approaching a teacher in this way, even though they would like to talk to someone. Under such circumstances, to encourage a student to come and talk is entirely acceptable and may be necessary.

DISCIPLINE AND COUNSELLING SKILLS

Part of the ascendant tutor's function is, as we have seen elsewhere, to deal with breaches of discipline. A tutor who is used to listening to students, rather than talking at them, and whose approach to students is courteous and respectful, may find that this kind of approach will achieve greater co-operation from the student than a more traditional confrontational approach. In a sense, much of the philosophy behind this book – and indeed behind pastoral care – is founded on such a view of staff-student interaction.

It should be stressed, however, that using a non-confrontational approach to discipline is not counselling. Full-time and trained counsellors rightly look askance at the use of counselling skills to manipulate clients. It is important that the tutor is clear in his own mind which activity he is engaged in, and if, during the course of an interview, he crosses the boundary from one to the other he needs to be aware that he has done so. For a student who is manipulated loses power over the relevant part of her life more than one who is coerced, since at least she cannot be coerced without knowing it. If counselling skills are employed in a disciplinary context, everything must be in the open, including the agenda – the purposes and the motives – of the tutor. Only if this is so is the student in a position to make genuine choices.

This is a complex issue since it is possible that a central motive of the tutor may be to make a student more amenable so that she accepts an uncongenial (perhaps unacceptable) situation. For some students – perhaps for many – school presents a quite inappropriate environment.

Most adapt to it, even though they may not benefit from what it has to offer. Some find adaptation more difficult, and it is such students who, having 'been a nuisance' all through their school career, suddenly become mature and responsible citizens and hold down a steady job once they leave school, to the amazement of some teachers.

Now it may be that pastoral systems in many schools exist in order to provide a means of manipulating such 'problem pupils' into co-operation with the institution. This is not a particularly worthy aspiration for any teacher, since it gives the institution a primacy which it ought not to have: after all, we are surely not going to argue that the students exist for the sake of the school. A defence of this function of pastoral staff is that the minority have to be humanely controlled in the interests of the majority. But this is in direct contradiction of the avowed aims of most comprehensive schools, namely, that the school endeavours to provide an appropriate education for all its students, developing and valuing whatever talents they have. Sacrificing those who do not fit in is not a principle to be found in the prospectus of any school with which I am acquainted, nor should any school work by such a maxim.

But they do, and the tutor needs to consider what his motives are. There seems validity to me in having as an objective providing assistance to cope with survival in an uncongenial institution to those students who require it. That is not the same as manipulating co-operation out of dissidents.

TIME

Teachers sometimes argue that they cannot employ a listening or non-directive approach to their students because they do not have the time. Counselling, they argue, requires that the counsellor gives up to the client as much time as it takes. Now I do not for a moment wish to deny that the multiplicity of demands upon teachers means that much of the time they have to undertake tasks at breakneck pace. What is not the case is that counselling needs unlimited time. Indeed, professional counsellors operate within very clear time boundaries, and most see advantages in sticking to them scrupulously, not only so that the next client is not kept waiting, but also because the client will generally make progress in her problem in between sessions and following the problem as far as it seems to go *now* may limit that process.

The problems which arise in teacher-counselling are as follows. First, when the student arrives with a problem, the tutor may not be able to counsel at that moment. 'May not be able' probably means that he has a lesson, and if he stays with his client, his class will be unattended. It is still a genuine choice, however, and there may be times when the tutor may feel that the client's problem is so urgent that the class will have to be left for a while. Or the client could accompany the tutor to the lesson. Usually, though, it is better to suggest a time when the tutor will be available, and it should be as soon as possible because the student may well feel this to be a rejection, and may not come back. Often, it is best to compromise: 'Look, I can only give you five minutes now and then I must go to a lesson.' The tutor should then listen for five minutes, if that is what the client wants, and at the end of that time suggest a time for a further interview.

Second, whereas a counsellor may be able to give up an hour a week to a client, the tutor will almost certainly be unable to do this – even if he commits free time to it. It is not a facility that the tutor can offer to the members of his group generally or he may find himself doing nothing else! It has to be said that if it appears that an hour a week for several weeks is what is required, then the tutor may have to consider referring the student to someone else.

If your school is fortunate enough to have a school counsellor, then whatever form of counselling the student requires will be readily available. Few schools at present are in this position, however, and most tutors will have to look elsewhere.

If the problem is a really serious one, social services may be willing to intervene, but they do not on the whole like open ended situations where there is no clear outcome. Child Guidance may be able to provide supportive counselling and will certainly be able to offer help where psychotherapy is deemed to be necessary. It is well worth consulting the school doctor or the student's own GP, who may be able to suggest a counselling service or an individual counsellor. Some surgeries have a counselling service, either officially or unofficially attached. Finally, in many areas there are counselling services which specialise in helping young people, such as the Brook Advisory Centres. The National Association of Young People's Counselling and Advisory Services, at 17–23 Albion Street, Leicester, LE1 6GD, will supply information on counselling services which are available.

However, much of the helpful listening which the tutor will be called upon to do can be achieved in one or perhaps two interviews. When the student arrives for counselling, whether the appointment is spontaneous or pre-booked, the time limits should be clearly spelt out. It is a good idea to have a clock on view, visible to both client and counsellor, so that the end of the interview comes as no surprise to the client. The time boundaries, once set, must be tightly adhered to. Once it is accepted that that is how you work, the end of the session is not seen as rejection. At the end of the session, book another one only if it is necessary. After all, you are on the spot, so it is not difficult if the student decides she needs to see you again.

Parkinson's Law – that work expands to fill the time available – operates in counselling as elsewhere, and the knowledge that only a short session is available will tend to mean that the client will explore her problem more rapidly. It is a good idea at the end of the session to give her some specific questions which can act as a focus for her to explore the problem further in her own time. This will mean that the counselling is not limited only to the period when the tutor and student are together.

Chapter 6

Recording and Reporting

One of the tasks of a pastoral care system is to keep records of, and to report on the progress of, students. Precisely what is recorded varies enormously from school to school. Some schools limit their recording to the reports which they send out to parents which comprise a comment and grades for each subject and an overall comment by the tutor; and 'incident records' which are held on file and which generally record disciplinary misdemeanours, such that a fat file will indicate a badly behaved student. At the other extreme, increasing numbers of schools are attempting to produce records of all the student's activities, in and out of school, often the product of a regular review negotiated between the student and her teachers.

On the whole, the fuller the records and the more the student has a say in what is said the better, though it should be stressed (as I did in the section on monitoring in Chapter 1) that it is possible for a school (or tutor) to spend so much time on recording that actually responding to situations tends to take a back seat. Recording is time-consuming and negotiating with students even more so, so that we have to be clear that the benefits justify it.

Record keeping

As a general rule, it is worth taking the attitude that most information recorded should be positive. There will, of course, be occasions when you will have to write a report of an incident which is to the detriment of the student involved – and such incidents do need to be recorded. But a frequent tendency in schools is to record *only* things which are to a student's discredit, so that her file is fat if she is often in trouble and thin if she is well behaved and hardworking. That this is the norm is an indictment of the thinking which, whatever they may claim, dominates the practice of schools, that they are so interested in failure and so uninterested in achievement. An attitude which sets the balance more towards success is therefore to be encouraged.

It is, of course, not possible to record every interaction involving a student, so it is a question of identifying those which are significant in building up a picture of the student. Anything which can be described as an achievement should be recorded. Examples of behaviour which seem to be indicators of personality will have to include incidents in which the student comes into conflict with staff under this heading, but once again instances of a positive nature must not be forgotten.

As with any evaluation, it should be borne in mind that success for one student might not be judged as particularly successful for another. Judgement should therefore be 'ipsative' (to employ a jargon term from Records of Achievement), that is, a student's success should be evaluated in terms of the particular student's past performance, rather than against the performance of other students or some norm. A very shy student who manages to contribute to a group discussion or a garrulous student who listens to the contributions of others without interrupting might be noted. Such is the raw material of any report or reference, which should include comment about improvement.

EXAMPLES

- **Membership of or special contribution to club or society in or out of school.**

- **Taking part in tutor group project.**

- **Special contribution to helping others.**

- **Incident revealing personal development.**

- **Organising activity.**

I do not want to give the impression that disciplinary misdemeanours should not be recorded. Clearly, they must. The response which the school makes to misbehaviour should be related to what the student has done in the past. Anyway, it is unfair to a student that an incident should lodge only in a teacher's memory where it may become exaggerated or distorted. A record of the incident will be a guard against this happening.

The format for recording will vary. Some schools operate a standard system for recording incidents, often using an incident slip. Sometimes these are slanted towards misdemeanours in the way they are set out and are unsuitable for any other kind of record. Formats are often restrictive anyway, and I favour a blank sheet of paper. The sheets should be of a standard size so that they cannot be missed when the tutor is checking through the file, but a blank sheet can be set out to suit the kind of comments that the tutor wants to make.

Of course, you may be constrained by the school's system. Worse, it may be, as we saw earlier, that you will not be the person responsible for recording your tutees' progress. You may even – though this is rare now – not have access to their records. There are schools which see records as so sensitive that the 'ordinary' teacher cannot be entrusted with them. However, it is more common for the records to be kept – in every sense – by the head of year/house and for the tutor to be allowed access if required. Occasionally, the tutor is actually responsible for both maintaining and holding the records.

If you have to work within a set system, it is a good idea to find out what latitude you have; how far you can modify the system to suit your own purposes. It is unlikely, for example, that you will be discouraged from including positive information. You may be in a school where you have the freedom to operate whatever recording system you like, or even to influence the system which the school employs.

Whatever is the precise situation in your school, it is generally possible and it is certainly desirable to write a brief report of any incident, achievement or significant contact in connection with a student in your tutor group. If the procedure demands it, then you can pass this to your pastoral head for filing. Some of the most caring and effective pastoral teachers try (and sometimes succeed) to keep all the data in their heads. The problem is that there is always the possibility that something gets forgotten, and anyway teachers get ill and even leave, and if there is no record such information becomes unavailable.

Clearly, any record should have the name of the student and the date of the record at the top of the sheet. It is a good idea to put a category at the top, too – discipline, achievement, contribution, for instance – or use different coloured sheets, so that the quantity of entries is not misinterpreted by someone who might not understand your system (or by you!).

Think about what information needs to be included. Don't put more than you need, because there simply isn't time, and if recording becomes too onerous the danger is that you won't do it at all. At the same time, be careful not to express yourself too eliptically: you (and others) will need to refer from time to time to what you have written, and it needs to be comprehensible.

The only kind of information that should be recorded is factual information. It is never a good idea to record conjecture, opinions or even inference unless they are absolutely implicit. Anything which can be challenged should be omitted. Partly, this is for the protection of the school: any records which are kept by the school are open to scrutiny by a parent (quite rightly), and inaccurate statements or unjustifiable remarks can lead to trouble for the school. Also, they can cause offence, which is unnecessary and damaging to the vital relationship between the school and the parent. Finally and most important, some kinds of remarks on a student's file can actually cause prejudice and lead to unfair treatment in school, and can affect treatment by prospective employers (for instance) subsequently.

So never write opinions or value judgements: stick to the facts, and be specific. Thus, 'Jonathan said, 'You're a bloody liar!' is better than 'Jonathan was rude'. Opinions and value judgements can always be challenged. It is particularly dangerous to speculate: 'Sheila's parents don't get on' might be a Well Known Fact, but it would take a lot of justifying if challenged.

Don't suppress information which is material to the incident you are describing, for any reason except confidentiality (which, as I have suggested in Chapter 5, is likely to be a factor only in exceptional circumstances). What appears unimportant now may have a bearing upon an incident in the future.

Recording should ideally be negotiated between tutor and student. At the very least, the student should be given the opportunity to see what you have written and comment on it – and the comments should be included with the record or as a part of it. A system which involves the keeping of records about students which the students are not aware of may be appropriate training for a closed society where secret records are kept on citizens, but the direction of public policy on this issue is towards more available information and less closed recording. Parents now have a legal right to see their children's records, and it makes sense that the students themselves should be able to do the same. Apart from that, any comments which the student might make about what is recorded is surely of significance, and should be recorded.

'On report'

There may be systems for recording already operating in your school and these should be exploited in the interests of your tutees. I do not only have in mind schools which are involved in Records of Achievement initiatives, but also much more traditional systems.

Most schools, for instance, employ a scheme of putting students 'on report'. This normally involves the student carrying a card to lessons which she presents to her teachers on arrival. The teacher is then able to make a comment (or sometimes just give a grade) concerning performance, effort, behaviour, or whatever, during the lesson. Often the report card is mainly employed as a punishment or threat to control unwanted behaviour or to act as a goad on students whose efforts are below what is expected.

But it is possible to use the report card more positively. One way of doing this is by encouraging students to see the card as a help to them, rather than as a system of control. To do this, it is advisable to seek the co-operation of your head of year/house because one essential element is that the report card is not used as a punishment; also, that it is not imposed, but that at the least its use is negotiated with the student, and at best students are only put on it at their own request. If possible, then, it can be a matter of policy that the card is used only with the active consent of the student; that its purpose is as a support to help the student to achieve certain goals; and that students can ask to go on report if they feel they need such support. This is not pie-in-the-sky: it is merely a matter of creating a climate in which the associations of the card are changed. Some students will want to be able to tell their friends that they are on report in order to justify their increased effort, since unfortunately making an effort in some peer groups is unfashionable. Others will be pleased to have '*Voluntary*' written on their report so that their parents can see that the card has not been imposed.

The approach described above will probably not be easy if you attempt to operate it in isolation in your own group, when the rest of the school sees the report card as part of the penal system. But another positive use of the report card *can* be operated individually. This involves influencing the kind of remarks which other teachers make on the report card, for example, by writing at the top of the card: 'Please write any positive achievement or contribution made by the student'. You should discuss this with your head of year/house before implementing it, of course. It is even possible to head the card: 'Please write *only* positive achievements or contributions made by the student'. This, of course, is more radical and some teachers may object to being prevented from making adverse comments, but when employed with students who have little respect for themselves it may be particularly effective.

Whatever use is made of report cards, though, it is possible and desirable for the tutor to discuss the previous day's reports with a tutee in a positive way. By this I mean that you should avoid any suggestion that the purpose of the debriefing is to identify areas where the student has fallen down and to reinforce staff disapproval. On the contrary, your function has to be to encourage and reward any signs of improvement which appear on the card. That doesn't mean not mentioning less creditable comments, or that you should not enquire into them, but that kind of attitude shouldn't provide the main focus for your discussions, and it should all be done in a friendly and non-judgemental way.

Report cards should be filed like other forms of record, and a note should be included with them about the context in which the student went on report.

Report writing

The tutor's role in the writing of reports is quite a responsible one in most schools. Even in the traditional grammar school setting, it was the practice for the form teacher to read through the subject reports and then write a summary report, which might include comments on social and personal factors and the contribution made by the student to extra-curricular activities.

This has changed little – nor should it – though the tutor is more likely to know (and be expected to know) the students well enough for such comments to be more comprehensive and indeed more dependable than might have been the case at one time.

The first task may be to extract the reports from the subject teacher and this is one of the areas of the tutor's role where not only tact but also firmness are needed. In difficult cases, the tutor – even the ascendant tutor – may need to call for the assistance of the pastoral head, since staff management is part of her role rather than that of the tutor.

You should not risk damaging your relationship with other staff in your efforts to get the reports in on time; in the end, it is not part of your job as a tutor (though, of course, it may be part of other roles you have) to manage staff.

Once you have the reports, you should check them through. You should be looking for a number of things. First, you should look for errors in spelling, punctuation and grammar. It is important that what goes out from the school should not leave any doubts as to whether the teaching staff themselves are properly educated, and in concentrating on the meaning everybody from time to time commits infelicities. Don't worry about matters of style which you dislike as long as they are not actually incorrect.

Second, you should look for any inaccuracies in the information given. Much of the factual content will, of course, be beyond your knowledge anyway, but there are times when you may be able to spot mistakes, particularly if you know the student concerned well. You may be surprised by remarks about her which don't fit your idea of her, and it is worth checking with the teacher (or with the student herself) to see what gave rise to them. Your view of the student may be incomplete – or the teacher may have got her muddled up with someone else!

Third, you need to try to spot trends in the report. What kinds of virtues are being noted? Is there any pattern to the criticisms? You can and should comment on anything of this kind, and indeed on any subject which is out of line with the overall picture.

Fourthly, you should have available a list of the achievements of the student which will not be mentioned by subject teachers, so that you can include them in the report, or at least make a reference which accommodates them. This would include club and society contributions, responsibility taken and help given in the tutor group, personal qualities which have been evident and so on.

In general, you should try to write balanced reports which recognise achievement and also give targets for the future. Writing a report on a student who has been heavily criticised is a difficult task for this reason. It is a bad idea to send a report out which is wholly negative. However aware a parent may be of her offspring's shortcomings, she will not enjoy reading someone else recounting them. The student herself is unlikely to react positively to a catalogue of her defects either, and to induce an improvement in her future performance is surely one of the objectives we are seeking. On the other hand, it is neither honest nor helpful to make it sound to a parent as if everything is fine when it isn't. It isn't fair to the student or her parents, since it doesn't give them the opportunity to consider the possibility of change, nor does it prepare them – if this is appropriate – for impending disaster. Equally, it is unfair to other students since, if all reports are good, how is a satisfactory student to know that she is satisfactory?

If your school has embarked on a Record of Achievement scheme, then your report writing will probably have been incorporated into it.I shall discuss this situation later in the chapter. The fact that for such a scheme what is to be written is negotiated with the student means that the student is more likely to be clear how much progress she is making. Even if your school is not involved in such a project, your pastoral head may be willing for you to negotiate with your tutees over the comments which you as the tutor write on their reports. She has then been a party to what is written and is much more likely to feel committed to the sense which they carry. Experience too shows that it is unlikely to be less honest.

Another approach which can be found in some schools now is to send out the student's own reports on herself with the staff reports. This also involves the student in her own assessment, and encourages the sense that her viewpoint is as valid as the teacher's.

Whatever method you use to establish the remarks which you are going to make, the format of the report which is always important is particularly so in the case of the 'bad' report. To enlist the parents' support, therefore, you should endeavour to find a positive way in. A report that begins with some recognition of the good qualities of the student is more likely to be attended to and read in a receptive frame of mind. It is also a good idea to finish on a positive note, leaving the reader feeling that your central interest is a concern for and appreciation of the needs of her child.

The 'meat' – the bad news – needs to go in the middle, therefore, making a 'bad news sandwich'. It is not a question of disguising the truth, but of avoiding the impression, which is only too easy to give, that the school is out to undermine the student. The bad news sandwich is a principle which can be employed in other contexts as well as the report – for example, if you need to write a letter to a parent about some aspect of the student's performance in school which has caused concern (though there are often advantages in meeting with the parent under such circumstances).

In general, it is advisable to work to a plan when writing reports, so that you don't leave anything out. I suggest the following:

TUTOR REPORT WRITING FORMAT
1. General statement of major positive qualities which have been apparent.

- Tracy has had quite a pleasing term, having approached most of her courses sensibly and with interest.

- Darren is a lively and cheerful person, whom I enjoy having in the tutor group.

2. Specific reference to subjects where there is (relative) achievement.

- Her work in Physics has been particularly impressive, and her History teacher has commented on the improvement in quantity and quality in her essay writing.

- He has show some improvement in English and his work in Art has again been first rate.

3. Specific reference to any difficulties or shortcomings.

- However, Tracy needs to approach Maths in a more serious frame of mind; her classwork in particular has sometimes been incomplete or casually done.

- I am disappointed, though, that Darren continues to find it difficult to put much into many of his courses. In Science, I have doubts as to whether he will be permitted to remain in the group next term, after the incident with the test tubes which we spoke about last week. It might be a good idea if we met again at the beginning of next term.

4. General statement of approach to social and cultural activities, with specific references where appropriate.

- Tracy continues to have a constructive attitude to school life, and is a lively member of the Discos Committee. It would be nice to see her lending her dramatic talents to the Drama Club if she felt she had time.

- I am pleased that Darren has rejoined the football team. His abilities are much needed there, and he has played well this term.

5. Comments on the development of personality.

- Tracy has matured this year, and has shown considerable responsibility when she has been given such opportunities – as a tuckshop server, for instance.

- I understand Darren's increasing frustration with school, but am concerned that he makes matters worse by challenging staff over trivialities. He still has three terms before he can leave and he is tending to have a damaging affect on the working atmosphere of some of the groups he is in.

6. Advice related to comments made so far.

- I hope Tracy can bring her usual good sense to bear in those subjects, like Maths and PE, which she likes less. I have discussed this with her and she feels that she has made more effort since half term.

- Darren and I have talked about what he wants to get out of school. I hope that we shall be able to arrange some work experience for him, but it is essential that he accepts the need for co-operation in the classroom.

7. **Personal comment to show tutor's affection for and contact with the student.**

   - I particularly enjoyed Tracy's company and her friendliness with younger students on the skating trip recently.

   - Darren continues to keep us amused in the tutor group, and I enjoy the arguments we have about politics.

Of course, these examples would be found in a school where the tutor was allowed a whole page for his comments. Where you have much less space you will need to conflate the content considerably, but the basic aim of getting across the information, while at the same time showing liking and concern for the student, remains the central object of the exercise.

SELF-EXPLORATION
How do you feel about the students in your tutor group? Make a list of the students you like, the students you dislike and the students you don't feel much about.
   Now ask yourself the following questions:

1. **Do you give more attention to the students you like? Do you give attention to the students you dislike mainly when they need to be reprimanded?**

2. **What strategies could you employ to make the students you dislike feel that you care about them?**

3. **How much attention do you give to the students you feel nothing much about? Do they have anything in common? How much do you know about them?**

What do you think your tutees think you are like? How much have you told them about yourself? Are you different in your tutor group from the way you are in lessons, with other staff, or at home? If so, how?

References

A reference is a particular kind of report which is written normally during the student's last year at school or after she has left. It is written specifically for a prospective employer or college or university, and focuses on those aspects of the student which make her suitable for the post or course for which she is applying.
   In many schools, references are written by the head teacher or sometimes by the head of year/house. But clearly the tutor is likely to

be best placed to undertake this kind of reporting, just as he is to undertake the kinds we have already discussed.

A first principle in writing references is to tell the truth. There is a temptation where the tutor is writing a reference for a student who has, say, been unreliable and awkward, but for whom he has a considerable affection, to suppress information or statements about her qualities because he wants her to get the job or college place. Apart from the question of integrity, there is a sound practical reason why this is not a good idea. This is that the tutor's influence as a writer of references only holds as long as what he has to say can be depended upon. It does not take long for a school to build up a reputation for sending unsatisfactory employees with good references. If the tutor can't be trusted, he is letting down students who really do deserve his highest praise.

A second principle is the opposite: the written reference should never be used as an opportunity to get back at a student who has been a problem at school. I have said that the tutor should not suppress the truth, but the truth need not be overstated and adverse comment should be balanced as far as possible by the recognition of good qualities. It is important to recognise that there are students – perhaps quite a lot of them – for whom the school is such an uncongenial environment that they adapt to it in ways which are seen as antisocial and disruptive. Some such students prove to be unsatisfactory employees, too, but others find the work environment totally different and respond well to it. We should not assume, therefore, that a difficult student will make an unsatisfactory employee. It is conceivable that a career could be nipped in the bud because of an unfavourable reference, and the tutor should not wish to bear the responsibility for that. There is, I believe, a duty to a student to recommend her as far as is consistent with the truth. Certainly, students themselves see 'getting us jobs' as one of the functions of the school, and though it is unrealistic of them to do so, it is not part of the school's task to thwart their aspirations without very good reason.

References differ from reports in that they are not intended to be seen by the student they concern, though there is no reason why the tutor should not show the reference to the student if he thinks that some purpose will be achieved by doing so. Since records have legally been open to parents, it has been possible for parents to specify that their children's references should be closed, thus forgoing the right to see them. This is on the basis – in my view, unwarranted – that teachers are less likely to tell the honest truth if they think parents are able to see what they have written.

What does affect the tone of what is written is not who will see it but for whom it is written. In the case of the reference, the intended reader is not the student or his parents, so the purpose is not to cause some particular behaviour in the student as is often the case with a report. In a report it makes sense to make constructive criticisms, to remark on even small improvements encouragingly, and above all to take very much into account the expectations which it is reasonable to have of the student, leading the teacher to comment adversely on an able student for not quite achieving her usual heights. In a reference, this approach is less appropriate. After all, the prospective employer needs by the end of the reference to have a fairly objective picture of the abilities and qualities of the student. Unlike the report, therefore, the first and last sentences need to introduce and sum up the main theme, rather than having to be positive.

On the whole, readers of references do not expect to read things along the lines of 'This student is totally unsuitable' or 'I would advise you not to employ her'. They are therefore prepared to read between the lines, and the tutor can write with this in mind. If he feels that the student is likely to be successful in the particular job, he can start 'I am writing to recommend June for this post' or 'I wish to support enthusiastically June's application'. If you are doubtful whether the student can be successful (you can never be more certain than this), you can begin 'I am writing concerning Helen's application for the post of ...'. You can continue with 'June has been a ——— student', where the blank can range from 'excellent' to 'pleasant' or 'co-operative' or 'steady'. The most unsatisfactory student might be described as having 'found some aspects of school difficult or uncongenial '.

The second paragraph should deal with examination successes or expectations. At present, these are the best – or at least the only trusted – indicator of ability available. There should follow comment in general terms concerning attendance and punctuality, which are of signal concern to the employer, and then a section dealing with the student's personal qualities, in particular referring to such aspects as reliability, capacity to take responsibility, getting on with others and honesty.

The last main section should deal with the student's activities outside the classroom. The tutor has recorded these regularly, as we have seen, but it is a good idea to check any changes or additions with the student anyway. List those undertaken in school first, followed by the others. Any particular achievements need to be mentioned first.

The final sentence should be a statement of the tutor's opinion of the student's suitability for the job. If you are doubtful, a formula such as 'I am unsure whether Helen would be suitable for this post' is appropriate, but generally you will be able to write 'I believe that June will prove to be an entirely satisfactory employee' or 'I feel that this post is one in which June will prove her worth'.

Many large employers send out forms which are rigid in format and require only the information which the employer regards as relevant to the job. They tend to stress certain character qualities, for instance. The problem there is that the referee may not know about the student's abilities in every area. For instance, it may be that she has not shown leadership qualities, but that might only mean that the opportunity has not arisen. It is best to leave a section blank if you are not sure – or even add a note to the effect that the student has not had the opportunity to show that quality – rather than commit yourself to something outside your experience.

Such forms always include space for the referee to write anything which seems to him especially important, and comments regarding activities and achievements outside the classroom are generally appropriate there.

Court reports

Court reports are the reports provided by the school to the Juvenile Court when a student is appearing charged with some offence. They are never used to help the magistrates decide the guilt or otherwise of the accused, but are produced after the verdict to assist in sentencing. Nevertheless, there is evidence (*School Reports in the Juvenile Court*, NACRO, 1984) to show that magistrates are heavily influenced by the report from the school, believing that '... teachers were likely to know a child better, and to see the child within *the normal everyday context of the school*' (Pask, 1984: his italics).

It is therefore essential that teachers writing or contributing to Court reports act circumspectly and professionally when they do so. Furthermore there are strong arguments for students to be consulted during their writing or at least to see the report before it goes to the Court – since there is at present no obligation on the Courts to disclose the contents of the report. It is also advisable if possible for the parents of the student to see the report as well.

The Court report is produced on a form. The format varies from area to area, but there is a fair amount of space and the mode of expression needs to be carefully thought out. The fact that it is so influential means that it is advisable for more than one person to be involved in its composition. One person (the tutor?) might draft it in pencil and a second – the head of year/house or the headteacher – read it through, amend and add to it, and then have it typed.

It is important to avoid emotive language – certainly derogatory language or any phrase which sounds dismissive. Opinions – if they must be expressed – need to be firmly grounded. There is a tendency for teachers, wishing to show that they know a student, to make character judgements on the basis of one incident. If you catch yourself doing this, it is better to cite the incident itself, and omit the generalisation. Hearsay should never be mentioned in any form. There is always a section about the family background of the student, and it is sometimes tempting to include 'knowledge' that you have, about the relationships in the family, for instance. Generally, it is best to take the line that teachers have an area of knowledge of the student concerned in which they are the experts, but that other professionals will be better able to give information on the student out of school. The social services department will have to make a social enquiry report in which such things as previous offences and family relationships will be mentioned.

Other reports

There are other kinds of reports which teachers may get asked to write from time to time: I have mentioned the multi-professional assessment form in Chapter 4, for example. The general rule is for the tutor to be clear in his mind *who the report is for*. Reports written for the student herself need to consider the effect that what is said may have, since they are almost certainly written with the intention of modifying or reinforcing behaviour. Many reports are not written for the student, however, and the tutor's approach to them should be quite different, as we have seen. It is important to be clear what function the report will have, why the report was requested in the first place, who will read it, what kind of action may be taken as a result of it, and so on.

Most reports can and should be shown to the student once the tutor has written them. In many cases it is helpful and constructive to their relationship for the tutor to discuss with the student what he intends to write. The student should certainly be aware that reports are being written and should have the opportunity to comment herself in most cases. The tutor should never show reports written to him by other members of staff or other agencies unless he has the permission of the writer to do so, though it is generally acceptable to pass on in appropriate language the substance of such a report.

The tutor should never be afraid to reject the format of a report form if he feels that it does not serve his purpose or might make him write something which he does not wish to say. This can be done either by attaching a slip of paper with his comments on, or by altering the wording on the relevant part of the form. He should not give grades unless he is confident about their meaning and satisfied that they are appropriate in the context.

Records of Achievement

In 1984, the Department of Education and Science published a policy document which stated that from 1990 the government intended that every student leaving school should take with her a Summary Record of Achievement, which would be the culmination of a process of recording what had taken place throughout the student's secondary school career. Though this date has since been deferred, so that while systems for recording achievement will be expected to be in place by 1990, schools will not be obliged to provide students with a leaving record until 1995, the DES is still committed to the introduction of Records of Achievement. This apparently simple scheme disguises what could be the most important development in secondary education since the introduction of comprehensive education – though it is possible that its impact will be much less than that.

The effect on the role of the tutor may be considerable, too – it certainly will be if it goes according to plan – so it is essential that the new tutor has some understanding of what is involved. The ascendant tutor will find that the development is in line with his view of the tutor's role as central to the pastoral system.

ISSUES INVOLVED IN RECORDS OF ACHIEVEMENT
Before we look at the impact which the development may have on the role of the tutor and is already having on some who are involved in pilot study schemes, we need first to examine the characteristics of Records of Achievement.

This is less than straightforward because there is no single pattern or blueprint for the organisation or format of the record or the process by which it is formed. The government set up nine initial pilot schemes to develop their own approaches, and other non-government schemes have followed. All have differences, some of which are considerable. However, it is possible to recognise a characteristic philosophy and some organisational generalisations can be made.

Before I go on to explore these, two distinctions need to be made. First, there is a distinction between the final record, or summary (sometimes 'summative') document, and the record which is constantly added to through the school life of the student, which is referred to as the formative document. The formative record is a lot longer for a start, and contains a lot more detail. It is envisaged that everything written in it would be the result of negotiation between the student herself and the teacher. It might include adverse comment, to which later statements concerning improvement could be related.

Second, there is a distinction to be made between the product (the record itself) and the process through which it comes to be made. Most of those developing Records of Achievement stress the greater significance of the process, because of the liberalising effects on the relationships between staff and students, the improvement in motivation and the contribution which they argue it would make to the personal development of the student. The idea is that teacher and student would join together to review the student's progress, and would record the results of their discussions, with the student having considerable control over what is said (some projects argue that the student should have as much or more say than the teacher on what is recorded).

Bearing these remarks in mind, I offer the following attempt to characterise the Records of Achievement movement. It is by its nature a simplification, but each point is argued, by at least some and in many cases most of the main practitioners and pilot projects, to be essential aspects of recording achievement.

Both the summary and the formative record should:

- be a record of achievements of all kinds, within the classroom and without, and possibly outside school as well;
- be for all students irrespective of ability;
- be written in language which is accessible to all who may read it, including parents, employers, and especially the students themselves;
- be the result of a continuous negotiated reviewing process between the student and teachers;
- probably include some kind of information about personal qualities and experience;
- possibly make some attempt to assess process or cross-curricular skills;
- seek to refer to criteria of achievement rather than relate to norms;
- list courses studied; and
- give a student view of intended possible careers/future courses.

The process of recording achievement should:

- be an integral part of the learning process;
- make a contribution to the motivation and personal development of the students;
- involve all teachers and departments;
- include discussion of negative as well as positive aspects of the student's life;
- be integrated as far as possible with existing reporting, recording and reference systems; and
- be part of the regular school routines.

The summary record, with which all students will leave, should:

- be a short document which will result from the formative record which has been built up over the student's period of schooling;
- include a record of examination results;
- include only positive statements; and
- be accredited by some outside body or consortium.

THE ROLE OF THE TUTOR IN RECORDING ACHIEVEMENT

It is clear that the recording of progress in individual subject areas will need to be negotiated between the student and a person who has detailed information about that progress, presumably the subject teacher. It makes no sense for one of the parties to be entirely ignorant of the factual basis of the negotiation. Nevertheless, there do seem to be several areas where the tutor will have a particular role to play.

The first is as a collector and collator of the subject rcords, which will need to be fed to someone and kept by that person. The tutor, with his particular overall concern for the student would seem to be the appropriate person for this task. The system might be for the subject reports to be held in departments until the end of the fifth year. This would make it possible for the student and subject teacher to refer to previous reports when they review progress. Somehow, however, both tutor and parents would need to receive a version of the record at various stages, just as at present reports are read by the tutor and then sent out to the parents. At the end of the student's school career, these records will then need to be distilled by negotiation to comprise the shorter summary record. This would presumably be the tutor's job, too.

Second, if any attempt is made to include some comment on the student's personal qualities and social competence, the tutor as the person who is closest to the student, who has known the student longest and who has known her in a social as well as an academic context would seem to be the person best placed to do this. It seems essential that some attempt should be made to deal with personal qualities. Apart from the fact that schools have traditionally made such comments on reports and references, to omit the personal would be to imply that schools aren't interested in personal development, which is less true at present than ever before.

Thirdly, there is an expectation that some record of personal experiences would be included in the Record of Achievement. In the short history of the movement, this is an area which has been quite well developed. Indeed, there are schemes – the Record of Personal Experience developed by Don Stansbury comes to mind most obviously – which include little else. The experiences to be recorded could include the traditional extra-curricular activities within school but could also contain experiences in other organisations and undertaken through the family or independently. Again, the tutor, whose overview of the student will include a knowledge of her life outside school, is best placed to do this.

The skills of reviewing which are clearly going to be needed by teachers in their role as subject teachers and as tutors need some mention. Reviewing in this context means considering past activities with a view to making a record of them. The skill of the teacher will be in making the student feel comfortable about speaking of her achievements and experiences as well as of her failures and shortcomings. She will need to be given ideas of the kinds of experience she should include since simply thinking of things may be a problem for some students, but the teacher needs also to give the student enough space so that she feels that her opinions about her experiences are valid. The fact that the teacher is often an authority figure is as much a problem in reviewing as it is in counselling, and indeed the two tasks have a lot in common. The difference is probably that while the purpose (the agenda) of counselling is open to the client to determine, in the case of reviewing there is a fixed task to be completed. The teacher under these circumstances, rather than tracking the student through whatever she wants to talk about, should aim to keep to the agenda of reviewing the experiences which are relevant to the record.

In the case of the subject teacher the agenda will be the experiences which the student has gone through in the course of her studies in that subject. In the case of the review of personal experiences, the brief is more diffuse since it is not clearly laid down what can count as approprate to the record. Nevertheless, we might identify two categories of experiences which should be included. On the one hand, the record needs to mention anything which can count as an achievement or which reveals worthwhile personal qualities. Membership of a sporting club or contribution to a community activity would count here. On the other hand, the record also needs to include any experience which might benefit the student. An interesting holiday or visit would be an example.

It seems clear that personal experiences will need to be expressed in sentences, perhaps in the student's own words or the tutor's, or an agreed compromise. There is, however, disagreement at present as to the precise way in which personal qualities might be recorded. The spectrum of opinion varies from ticking boxes which relate to qualities judged by the designer of the form to be important, on what might be termed the right wing of the movement, to writing sentences which are 'made-to-measure' for the particular student, on the left wing. In between come word- and sentence-banks which attempt to bring a measure of standardisation to the record. Such standardisation may be spurious if personal qualities are as individual as one might suppose. On the other hand, the 'made-to-measure' approach puts a great deal of responsibility on the capacity of the tutor and student to put what they think into clear language.

Fortunately, the tutor himself is unlikely to have to make the decision about which system is the most satisfactory, since he will have to work within a system which is at least to some extent standardised nationally.

As we have seen, the assessment of personal qualities has always been a task which teachers have attempted, both in reports and references, and I have already argued that the tutor is best placed to take it on. However, just as some teachers prefer to deal in facts when writing references – what the student has done rather than what she is – this is a line which might be taken in recording achievement, though many schemes do aim to produce a direct statement of the qualities of the student as part of the summary record. The formative record, which allows for the possibility of unfavourable comment, is also expected to include such assessment, which would allow for the possibility of statements regarding character development.

The questions which will need to be answered are how the reviewing process can be integrated into existing tutor patterns, and how the recording process can be integrated into existing reporting and recording processes. Clearly, such integration is necessary otherwise an inordinate amount of extra time would have to be found if a school were to take on records of achievement. Apart from that, recording achievement will involve – or indeed improve upon – many of the operations which at present take place under existing systems, and there is clearly no sense in duplicating those tasks.

Chapter 7

Your School: Special Problems

It is impossible not to recognise that the ideas contained in this book are more easily achieved in an institution where the prevailing ethos is in tune with them, where all staff from the head teacher onwards approach their relationships with students similarly, and where the tutor is expected to have an ascendant role.

However, it is too easy to decide that because many staff do not share a particular standpoint the tutor has to put his own ideas on one side and fit in with the practices of the majority, or to feel that he has to operate as a tutor within the existing constraints. Change in schools begins with individuals, and though I would certainly concede that commitment from the top is to say the least helpful, 'bottom up' developments are likely to be more deeply founded and more thoroughgoing.

If the individual tutor is going to make the first tentative steps towards change by operating in a particular way as an individual, then clearly he needs to have a thorough understanding of the institution as it is. In this chapter, I want to consider some of the problems which may confront the new tutor, and suggest some ways of approaching them.

The Hidden Curriculum

We tend to think that a school is bound to have a clear conception of the knowledge, skills, attitudes and values which it intends to transmit to its students. This is only partly true. If a school includes mathematics in the curriculum, then the Maths department will need to have worked out what they want the students to know and what skills they want them to acquire, and the same is true in any department. But beyond the (hopefully) systematically planned course contents, there is a whole range of learning, much of which will never even appear in the prospectus, even less be stated as part of the curriculum. Indeed, in many schools much of the learning to which I am referring is unconsciously and inadvertently taught, and some of it the school would not wish to teach if it were aware of it.

This 'hidden curriculum' is a facet of Marshall McLuhan's dictum that the medium is the message, that the way something is taught may be more fundamental and significant learning than the content. Thus, we might define it as the aspects of the school organisation, ethos and relationships which are learnt by the students as they adapt to operating within the school.

It is not difficult to see that this learning might include all kinds of things which the school authorities have no intention of teaching, such as which is the best entrance for a student to use if she's late or which teachers never check up on homework. But it will also include more fundamental learning, which may be difficult for the school to control but which it is important for it at least to be aware of. It may be that in fact the Hidden Curriculum should not be hidden at all, but should be a clearly articulated aspect of school policy, but this is easier said than done, and it is certainly not the same as some of the worthy but insubstantial verbiage to be found in many a school prospectus.

The most important factor in the Hidden Curriculum is the nature of the informal interactions between student and teacher. The way in which students are addressed by teachers is the clearest indication of the quality of a school which it is possible to find on a brief visit, and the second clearest indication is the way that the students address the teachers. At best it is that they address each other as any adult might address any other. There should be no obvious sense that one is in a position of authority over the other. It should be clear that each respects the other.

Some people are fond of asserting (and this is a view to be found expressed from time to time in the popular press) that pupils don't respect teachers any more, and certainly it is true that automatic respect for the role is much less a factor in school relationships. But the notion of respect for each other as people is by no means dead, and the most effective way of teaching it is by example. Students who see teachers using their position rather in the way that bullies use theirs will only learn that when you have power over someone else it is all right to do as you like.

A second aspect of relationships which can be seen as part of the Hidden Curriculum is the approach taken to control. In a school where 'The school rules' is a lengthy document, and where rules seem to circumscribe every place, time and possible type of action, students may have real difficulty when they find themselves in situations where the precepts are not clearly delineated (for instance, while staying in a hotel on a school holiday or on a visit to the theatre), and may behave inappropriately – 'badly'. They may find also the lack of clear guidelines when they leave school difficult to handle. If the rules are never justified – and in some cases perhaps appear incapable of justification – it is hard for students to come to understand the function which social rules of all sorts have in society. One rule seems as arbitrary as another, so that there is less chance of students developing a moral sense for themselves.

A school which takes a generally punitive line towards rule-breaking is educating its students to accept that punishment is the normal reaction towards deviance – not (to make it absolutely clear what I mean) just a natural reaction towards wickedness, which is an intelligible position– since many of the rules which are a normal part of life in many schools have nothing to do with wickedness or moral behaviour at all. For instance, a common rule is that students have to leave the school buildings and stay outside during breaks. Breaking this rule in itself hurts no-one: the only crime is disobedience. The rule against smoking is similar for those students over 16, unless approaches to smoking are part of a whole school anti-smoking policy; usually, however, no smoking rules in school are part of what amounts to a game which students play with teachers, and which the teachers win if a student gets caught. They can be no more than that as long as teachers smoke in school.

Rules like these are teaching more about the nature of power than anything. They fit into a context in which discipline ceases to be a means to civilised community living where the rights of individuals are weighed against their responsibilities to other individuals, but becomes an end in itself. The school becomes a place which by its nature causes deviance, since it is virtually impossible for a student to avoid breaking some rules some of the time. In such a context, teachers need to remember that breaking the rules does not imply wickedness – perhaps it implies ineptitude.

A humane school tries to ensure that the only rules are those which can be justified – perhaps even which justify themselves (since it is *possible* to justify almost any rule). Most such rules will concern behaviour designed to ensure that every member of the school is able to carry on her legitimate business without hindrance.

From such a system, students may have the opportunity to learn that rules contribute to individual freedom and the running of institutions and communities in the interests of their members.

A third element in the Hidden Curriculum concerns the questions which teachers ask students. John Holt (1969) and others have recognised that many of the questions which teachers ask are not just closed but have only one correct answer. Thus, students learn not to think what might be a sensible answer to a question but to guess which answer the teacher has in her mind. It is not that she says 'no' when another answer is given. She may generously say 'yes', but even if she manages not to say it in the doubtful tone which means 'Er yes: that is to say, er no', she shows that the student is not there by continuing to look for other answers until she gets the one she is looking for. Students learn from this that it doesn't matter what is true or rational; it only matters what the authority figures want for an answer. They also learn that there is only one right answer to a question. All of this is of course anti-educational, except in the sense that learning dates in history lessons is educational.

Obviously, there are other elements of the Hidden Curriculum. Every interaction between people, whether between staff and students, staff and staff (and this includes clerical, kitchen and cleaning staff, too) or student and student plays a part in the formation of the students' view of the organisation of society, of normal behaviour and of relationships.

The tutor's role in all this is a highly significant one, partly because of the degree to which he is able (obliged) to be less formal in his relationships with his students, partly because of his role as moral arbiter and social guide to his tutees, and partly because of the influence he has through the continuity which he can provide as the student goes through the school. (Though a few schools still have no policy for continuity in this respect, most year systems involve the tutor 'rolling', that is, moving up with his tutor group, for at least more than one year.)

In a school where the Hidden Curriculum seems to be teaching the arbitrariness of power and authority, that does not mean that you have to subscribe to it. It is necessary in all aspects of teaching to find out how your personality and values can be adapted to the job, not to change to become like another teacher. However, ploughing a lone furrow is hard work. It is best to spend time identifying other staff who share your ideas – there are always some – and gain support and advice from them. Your contribution towards the humanity of the Hidden Curriculum can be to ensure that all your interactions with students convey a respect for them, through your courtesy and your willingness to value what they have to say. This is something you can do within any institution, whatever its prevailing ethos.

Tutor ascendancy in a 'tutor subordinate' school

As I have already suggested, it is not really practicable to expect the pastoral head, the head of year or house, to 'do' all the caring for her year or house herself. If she tries to, she will amost certainly fail, since the numbers for whom she must care mean that she will only be able to care properly for a few – the deviant minority, probably – or, less usually, that she will care for them all inadequately.

However, there are schools – lots of them – where this is the role which middle management is expected to carry, and you may be in one of them. If the tutor is regarded as subordinate rather than ascendant in a school then the tutor has to take whatever opportunities he can to make himself such an indispensable pastoral resource that his pastoral head will be more or less compelled to exploit him. There are a number of ways in which he can do this, and it is best to use them all if this object is to be achieved.

First, he can regard the mundane administrative tasks as a useful pastoral opportunity rather than something which is getting in the way. We considered this approach in Chapter 1. Apart from the fact that it provides a chance to make contact with his tutees, to exploit positively a potentially unrewarding task is good for his own morale. What is more, in taking every opportunity to get to know his tutees better, he is building relationships with them which may be of use to the pastoral unit later, and he is developing his knowledge of his tutees which make him a resource for his pastoral head, as a repository of information.

Second, he can ask his pastoral head if she will allow him to 'see this one through', ie follow a particular case all the way himself, rather than referring it 'up'. For the sake of diplomacy, and to benefit from her experience, he should discuss what action should be taken at each juncture. Every time he is able to do this, he is developing his own pastoral experience, and whenever he does it successfully he is showing himself to be someone who can be trusted to take on such responsibilities.

A third method might be to initiate action, but to ask for permission from the pastoral head to do this: for instance, 'Do you mind if I contact her parents about this?' At this stage, he may have to use his own time, but it is not unreasonable, once he has shown that his taking on such tasks saves time rather than creating problems for the pastoral head, to expect some support – perhaps that the pastoral head take part of a lesson for him while he makes the call.

Finally, to make himself a resource for his tutees, the good tutor needs to know all about the school of which he is a part and how it works, because this is information which his tutees will be able to use and they will come to rely on him. If a tutor works so well with his group that his tutees come to trust him, then he has made himself an indispensable resource. A pastoral head who does not value and use the tutor who is trusted by his tutees is not doing her job properly.

It is important for aspiring ascendant tutors to understand that pastoral heads may not altogether like the idea of passing over the bulk of direct pastoral care to the tutor. It means much less contact with children, for one thing. It means learning new and unfamiliar skills for another. It means losing that role in which even the most sympathetic head of house or year feels a sneaking pride, of the teacher who can 'handle difficult kids'. This last role actually works against the disciplinary effectiveness of the rest of the staff, since a child may perceive that she is sent to the pastoral head when other staff are finding her difficult, so she takes less notice of other staff. Referral to her tutor when she is 'a problem' is much more effective: all staff are tutors to someone, and are consequently perceived as the people who can 'handle difficult kids' by their own tutees. Nevertheless, it can be a help to use your pastoral head for help and advice, and asking her for such support is a good way of enlisting her co-operation.

Building a reputation as a tutor who can be trusted takes time. Many senior teachers take the view that tutors should not be able to contact parents directly, for example, because they believe that they will act tactlessly and cause more problems than they solve. But tact is not a monopoly of the experienced, nor do deputy heads (or even – dare I say it? – heads) always act wisely and circumspectly. In the end, it is a combination of confidence and those counselling qualities of empathy, congruence and unconditional positive regard which is really effective.

A final difficulty is that in all but the most tutor ascendant schools, the tutor is unlikely to be given much if any time to a carry out the kind of duties I have been discussing. He is therefore dependent upon his pastoral head for any time that he may be given – unless he is willing to use his preparation and marking time or his own free time. As schools come to see the value of the ascendant tutor, we may hope that they will make protected pastoral time available to all tutors. For the time being, it can only be argued that it is to the benefit of all teachers that use of time in forming and maintaining relationships, not only with the students themselves, but with their parents, with their subject teachers, with the pastoral head and with outside helping agencies will in the end pay dividends.

Handling unsympathetic colleagues

The commonest unsympathetic colleague is the teacher who believes that the only way to deal with young people is arbitrarily, punitively and confrontationally. Such teachers are unlikely to put it in such terms. They are much more likely to accuse the tutor of being 'soft'.

It is much easier to say that we should not allow this epithet to sting us into acting 'tough' than it is to follow this advice. Moreover, the tutor should make certain that he is not justifying lack of firmness by allowing it to masquerade under the label of 'humane treatment'. It is not humane to avoid laying down clear guidelines, and certainly not humane to fail to stand by them when they are infringed.

What the tutor needs to demonstrate is that working within his own methods, he can be as effective as anyone else. The question is what criteria of effectiveness are we going to be prepared to accept? For here we come across the moral issue of whether manipulation is actually more humane than bullying. If the only criterion which will be accepted by our 'tough' colleague is whether some undesirable behaviour stops or not, then it may be that she will only be satisfied if the tutor can persuade (by whatever means) the student concerned to stop. She will not be satisfied by being informed that the student's behaviour is justified – even if it is.

She will certainly not be interested in statements along the lines of 'David has got to work through this situation in his own way', which will only go to confirm her in her suspicion that the tutor is 'soft'.

Fortunately, the two demands, that of the school and that of the student, quite often coincide in this kind of situation. The fact is that if David continues to, say, cause disruption in lessons, he will continue to get into trouble. It will make for an easier life for David if he modifies his behaviour, and will also make for an easier life for the teacher concerned and for the school authorities.

We have to accept, though, that the student may not share this perception. Sadly, the rewards in school for some students are few, as they have long since come to believe that they are deficient in the abilities favoured, which tend to be academic. The response of some of these students is to be disruptive, since they have discovered that this kind of behaviour brings them a notoriety which feels like kudos. It is difficult to persuade such students that it is in their interests to conform, since this is to take away their only route to a kind of self-respect.

Even with these students, however, if the tutor can behave with total congruence – sincerity – he may be able to gain the respect of the student sufficiently so that the attention she gets from him may compensate for the loss of notoriety, and she may come to value the praise she gets when she copes in more socially acceptable ways.

What is unfair in the kind of situation we have been considering, where a humane and non-confrontational approach is being compared with a more traditional and punitive stance, is, first, that neither is always successful, and second, that the short term and therefore more evident effects tend to be seen with the punitive methods, though it may be that in the long term, by hardening attitudes and increasing alienation, they actually work less effectively in producing conforming behaviour. Third, if we consider the effects of a punitive approach on the student herself, rather than from the point of view of the institution, it is difficult to ignore the sense that she has been sacrificed for order. The result is that the goal at the humane end seems sometimes wider than that at the other end.

However, in practice, it is rarely the case that individuals are as stereotyped as I have implied. The most liberal staff have their moments of vengeance, and often teachers who have the reputation of arbitrariness can be surprisingly sympathetic to an individual student's situation. It is worth the tutor trusting his colleagues and sharing with them his view of the situation. In a sense this book is all about trust since it is only in a school where teachers are regarded as professionals who can be trusted to deal sensitively with a range of difficult situations that the tutor will be able to be ascendant. Most teachers do like young people and are prepared to consider a situation from their point of view, if they have it explained to them in a down-to-earth way which avoids sentimentality. The central solution to handling unsympathetic colleagues is therefore to avoid erecting or maintaining barriers with them just as much as with students, and in a sense to refuse to accept that colleagues are or can be unsympathetic. Labelling in any sphere is the greatest barrier builder.

The head and his role

Many teachers work in schools where they feel, rightly or wrongly, that the head teacher does not share their own philosophical position, or fails to value their contribution, or is too removed from the students or the staff or both, or any number of similar complaints.

It is certainly important what the head thinks or does. She can affect the overall direction and morale of the school by holding to a clear line and encouraging it to be shared by her staff. It is also important that she recognises, values and exploits the talents and experience of her staff.

151

These are positive leadership qualities which can make a great difference.

However, the fact that a head is not successful in making staff feel that they are part of a working commitment, either because her stance is unclear or because it is uncongenial, does not mean that individual teachers cannot develop a stance of their own and work within that. In all schools there are teachers who 'do not fit in' but who work successfully and are respected for what they do.

The role of the head teacher as far as the tutor is concerned varies. Some heads like to work close to the ground, to discuss individual cases with the tutor and both tap their knowledge and oversee their functioning. Others work only through middle or even senior management, with a clear hierarchical structure that is rarely by-passed. On the whole, it tends to be useful to the tutor if he can communicate with the head directly, partly in order to understand the kind of line she favours and partly because there are times when the head's support is a considerable advantage – particularly when something goes wrong and he needs to be rescued! That the head understands that the tutor is working on the whole sensitively and conscientiously can pay dividends when the tutor has done something crass or has simply forgotten some task. This applies to the tutor's relationship with whichever rung of management he has to deal with anyway, but is most important with the head simply because she is the final arbiter.

The tutor needs to be careful to maintain his closest relationship with his head of year/house, since this is the line of communication which will benefit his tutees most. Nevertheless, a tutor who has a route to the top is of more use to his tutees than one who does not – though he should not use it too much and should keep his head of year/house informed of what he is doing, in this as elsewhere. It is a matter of keeping open as many lines of communication with as many people who can be of help to the tutor and his tutees as possible.

References

Aspy, D N and Roebuck, S N (1977) *Kids Don't Learn From People They Don't Like.*

Clemett, A J and Pearce, J S (1986) *The Evaluation of Pastoral Care* Blackwell, Oxford.

Culshaw, J and Eustance, A (1983) *Towards a Suggested Strategy of Co-ordination for Teachers* Liverpool LEA.

Hamblin, D H *The Teacher and Pastoral Care* (1978) Blackwell, Oxford.

Hargreaves, D H (1967) *Social Relations in a Secondary School* Routledge and Kegan Paul, London.

Hargreaves, D H, Hester, S K and Mellor, F J (1975) *Deviance in Classrooms* Routledge and Kegan Paul, London.

Hopson, B, and Scally, M *Lifeskills Teaching* (1981) McGraw Hill, London.

Holt, J (1969) *Why Children Fail* Penguin, London.

Marland, M (1974) *Pastoral Care* Heinemann, London.

NACRO Working Group (1984) *School Reports in the Juvenile Court* NACRO, London.

Pask, R (1984) School reports to the Juvenile Court, in *Pastoral Care in Education* Blackwell, Oxford, November.

Truax, C and Carkhuff, R (1967) *Toward Effective Counseling and Psychotherapy* Aldine, Chicago.

Further Reading

Baldwin, J and Wells, A (1979) *Active Tutorial Work* Blackwell, Oxford

Blackburn, K (1975) *The Tutor* Heinemann, London.

Blackburn, K (1983) *Head of House, Head of Year* Heinemann, London.

Bulman, L and Jenkins, D (1986) *The Pastoral Curriculum* Blackwell, Oxford.

Button, L (1981) *Group Tutoring for the Form Teacher* Hodder & Stoughton, London.

Haigh, G (1975) *Pastoral Care* Pitman, London.

Hamblin, D H (1978) *The Teacher and Pastoral Care* Blackwell, Oxford.

Hamblin, D H (1981) *Problems and Practice of Pastoral Care* Blackwell, Oxford.

Hamblin, D H (1981) *Teaching Study Skills* Blackwell, Oxford.

Hamblin, D H (1986) *A Pastoral Programme* Blackwell, Oxford.

McGuiness, J B (1982) *Planned Pastoral Care* McGraw-Hill, London.

Jones, A (1979) *Counsellors in Practice* Kogan Page, London.

Marland, M (1974) *Pastoral Care* Heinemann, London.